Nahum, Habakkuk, Zephaniah

The Lord Delivers His Faithful

"The righteous shall live by his faith."

Habakkuk 2:4b

Albert B. Collver III

CONCORDIA PUBLISHING HOUSE • SAINT LOUIS

3558 S. Jefferson Avenue, St. Louis, MO 63118-3968
1-800-325-3040 · www.cph.org

Written by Albert B. Collver III

Edited by Robert C. Baker

This publication may be available in braille, in large print, or on cassette tape for the visually impaired. Please allow 8 to 12 weeks for delivery. Write to Lutheran Blind Mission, 7550 Watson Rd., St. Louis, MO 63119-4409; call toll-free 1-888-215-2455; or visit the Web site: www.blindmission.org.

1 2 3 4 5 6 7 8 9 10 19 18 17 16 15 14 13 12 11 10

Contents

History	*Date (BC)*	*Scripture Reference*
Jonah preaches against Nineveh	**793–753**	2 Kings 14:25
Hezekiah repairs the temple	**715**	2 Kings 18
Reign of Manasseh (Judah)	**696–642**	2 Kings 21:1–18
Fall of Thebes, the upper Egyptian capital	**663**	
Nahum prophesies against Nineveh	**c. 663–612**	
Zephaniah written; Reign of Josiah (Judah)	**640–609**	2 Kings 22–23:30
Josiah purges the high places	**629**	2 Kings 23:1–20
Jeremiah called to be a prophet	**628**	Jeremiah 1:1–19
Fall of Nineveh	**612**	
Nebuchadnezzar besieges Jerusalem	**605**	2 Kings 24:10ff.
Habakkuk written	**c. 605**	
Nebuchadnezzar takes captives	**599**	2 Kings 25:1–7
Jerusalem temple destroyed	**587**	2 Kings 25:8–17

An Outline of Nahum

Nahum is a prophet of comfort who preaches that the Lord will deliver His people from her enemies. Nahum is dated within a fifty-year span between the fall of Thebes, 663 BC, and the fall of Nineveh, 612 BC. Nahum provides one of the best examples of classical Hebrew poetry, exceeded only by Isaiah. The contents of Nahum can be readily divided into two parts. Part 1 consists of chapter 1, which contains a magnificent hymn of praise describing the Lord as the divine warrior. Incidentally, Habakkuk concludes with a similar hymn. Part 2 contains chapters 2–3, which describe the Lord's judgment of Nineveh.

Luther writes of Nahum, "Thus there is nothing else here but the doctrine of faith. You see, he is teaching us to trust in God and especially when we despair of every human protection, every human power and planning, to believe that the Lord is close to His people and protects them against the assaults of every foe, no matter how powerful such foes may be, etc. But there is need here for a faith that believes that" (AE 18:282).

Superscription (1:1)

I. The Divine Warrior (1:2–15)
   a. Poem of the Lord's Wrath and Care (1:2–8)
   b. Doom for Nineveh and Deliverance for Judah (1:9–15)

II. The Lord's Judgment of Nineveh (2:1–13)
   a. Nineveh Besieged and Pillaged (2:1–10)
   b. Lion's Den Comparison (2:11–13)

III. Woe over Nineveh (3:1–19)
   a. Woe to the City of Blood (3:1–3)
   b. Nineveh Compared to a Prostitute (3:4–7)
   c. Nineveh Compared to Thebes and Cush (3:8–11)
   d. Final Taunts (3:12–19)

An Outline of Habakkuk

Habakkuk records a dialogue between the prophet and the Lord. Yet unlike other prophetic books, rather than the Word of the Lord coming to the prophet, the prophet goes to the Lord on behalf of the people. Because Habakkuk questions the Lord about evil in the world, some have called him "the philosopher prophet."

Luther writes that Habakkuk "is a comforting prophet whose mission was to strengthen and to sustain the people, so that they would not despair of the Christ's coming, no matter how difficult the situation might appear to be. To this end he employed all means and methods to fortify their faith in the promised Christ in their hearts" (AE 19:155).

Superscription: The Oracle of Habakkuk (1:1)

I. The Lord's Justice? (1:2–2:5)
   a. Habakkuk's First Complaint: How Long Shall I Cry for Help? (1:2–4)
   b. The Lord's Answer: Look and Be Amazed (1:5–11)
   c. Habakkuk's Second Complaint: Why Do You Tolerate the Wicked? (1:12–2:1)
   d. The Lord's Answer: Write Down My Revelation (2:2–5)

II. The Lord's Justice Is Certain: Woe to the Evildoer (2:6–20)
   a. Woe to Him Who Reaps but Does Not Sow (2:6–8)
   b. Woe to the Greedy (2:9–11)
   c. Woe to Him Who Builds on Bloodshed (2:12–14)
   d. Woe to the Drunk and Violent (2:15–17)
   e. Woe to the Idol-maker (2:18–20)

III. Habakkuk's Prayer (3:1–19)

An Outline of Zephaniah

Zephaniah is sometimes considered the neglected prophet of the seventh century BC. The superscription in verse 1 identifies Hezekiah as the great-great-grandfather of Zephaniah. Most scholars believe that he wrote before Josiah's reforms (about 629 BC). Zephaniah provides an almost perfect example of the classical three-part prophetic outline: 1. Judgment against Judah; 2. Gentile Oracles; 3. Promise and Restoration. Zephaniah's proclamation of judgment, remnant, and restoration serves as a segue to the New Testament period. He points ahead to Christ's kingdom and the Church.

Luther writes on Zephaniah: "This prophet is quite simple and clear, since he himself indicates the purpose and time of his prophecy. Among the minor prophets, he makes the clearest prophecies about the kingdom of Christ" (AE 18:319).

Superscription (1:1)

I. The Day of the Lord Is a Day of Judgment (1:2–3:8)
   a. The Lord Judges Judah (1:2–2:3)
   b. The Lord's Wrath against the Nations (2:4–15)
      i. West—Philistia (2:4–7)
      ii. East—Moab and Ammon (2:8–11)
      iii. South—Cush (2:12)
      iv. North—Assyria (2:13–15)
   c. Jerusalem Judged (3:1–8)

II. The Day of the Lord Is a Day of Restoration (3:9–20)
   a. Conversion of the Nations (3:9–10)
   b. Remnant of Judah Saved (3:11–13)
   c. Song of Victory (3:14–20)

Introduction to Nahum, Habakkuk, and Zephaniah

Nahum, Habakkuk, and Zephaniah appear in the section of the Old Testament known as the Minor Prophets, or "The Book of the Twelve." All three of these books were written in the seventh century BC. There are some interesting features of these books. Nahum begins with a divine warrior hymn, while Habakkuk ends with one. Habakkuk deals with theodicy, asking why God allows people to suffer. In a way, Zephaniah summarizes the content of all the previous Minor Prophets.

Lesson 1

The Divine Warrior

Nahum preached against Nineveh about a century after Jonah. When Jonah preached, Nineveh repented in sackcloth and ashes. However, Nineveh did not heed Nahum's warning; it was defeated by Babylon a few years after Nahum's ministry was completed. Nineveh returned to its wicked ways by trusting in its wealth and power. The city even contemplated attacking Judah, the remnant of Israel.

Judah, the small kingdom of the people of God, was to hear the words of Nahum and take comfort that the Lord God would save them. From a human standpoint, Nineveh, the great kingdom of Assyria, could easily destroy the insignificant land of Judah. Yet, just as all human help and ability failed, Judah learned that the Lord would be faithful to His promises.

Adversity Leads to Repentance and Trust

Martin Luther wrote that Nineveh "turned to repentance, the punishment was deferred; but such are the hearts of men that when the punishment ceased, so did the repentance. They slipped back into the same wickedness under which they had labored before" (AE 18:281).

1. How do judgment and adversity lead a person to repentance?

2. How does the removal of all human help, protection, power, and planning drive us to trust in the Lord and His promises?

The Lord's Wrath and Care

Read Nahum 1:1–8.

3. Read Isaiah 13:1. What do the similarities between Isaiah 13:1 and Nahum 1:1 tell us about how the Lord works?

4. Read Exodus 20:5–6; 23:22; and 34:6–7. In the Exodus 34 passage, the Lord reestablishes His covenant with His people after the golden calf incident. How does Nahum's allusion to this comfort the Lord's people?

5. How do these verses testify to the Lord's power and wrath?

Doom for Nineveh and Deliverance for Judah

Read Nahum 1:9–15.

6. How do people "plot against the LORD"?

7. The Scriptures frequently compare sin to drunkenness. Why is sin like drunkenness?

Nahum 1:13 says that the Lord will "break His yoke from off you." In Matthew 11:30, Jesus says, "For My yoke is easy and My burden is light."

8. How does hearing that the Lord's enemies will be defeated make your yoke or burden light?

God's Word for Today

At first glance, the message of Nahum seems disconnected from the world we live in today. The Assyrians are long gone as a world power. Yet we also feel oppression in our lives and are comforted by hearing that the Lord will deliver His people. Even more importantly, the prophets, including Nahum, testify to Christ Jesus, who has delivered us from sin, death, and the power of the devil. Regarding Nahum 1:15, Martin Luther wrote, "In this way we are all convinced that there is not any one prophet who did not blend something of his prophecy with the coming of Christ and the grace to be revealed through Christ. . . . There is no other passage in this prophet which we can take as related to Christ except this one" (AE 18:295).

9. Read John 12:3. Mary anointed Jesus' feet with perfume as an act of worship, quite literally finding His feet beautiful. How was this prophesy about the "feet of him who brings good news" fulfilled in Jesus?

10. Read Romans 10:15. St. Paul asks, "How are they to preach unless they are sent?" Today, pastors are those who "preach the good news." Why is it important that the Church continues to prepare, train, and send pastors into the world?

In Closing

Encourage participants to begin the following activities:

- Consider how the destruction of the Lord's enemies is good news for His people.
- Pray that the Lord of the harvest send workers into the field (Luke 10:2).
- Read Nahum 2 to prepare for the next section.

Sing or read together "Our Father, Who from Heaven Above" (*LSB* 766):

1. Our Father, who from heav'n above
Bids all of us to live in love
As members of one family
And pray to You in unity,
Teach us no thoughtless words to say
But from our inmost hearts to pray.

3. Your kingdom come. Guard Your domain
And Your eternal righteous reign.
The Holy Ghost enrich our day
With gifts attendant on our way.
Break Satan's pow'r, defeat his rage;
Preserve Your Church from age to age.

6. Forgive our sins, Lord, we implore,
That they may trouble us no more;
We, too, will gladly those forgive
Who hurt us by the way they live.
Help us in our community
To serve each other willingly.

8. From evil, Lord, deliver us;
The times and days are perilous.
Redeem us from eternal death,
And, when we yield our dying breath,
Console us, grant us calm release,
And take our souls to You in peace.

9. Amen, that is, so shall it be.
Make strong our faith in You, that we
May doubt not but with trust believe
That what we ask we shall receive.
Thus in Your name and at Your Word
We say, "Amen, O hear us, Lord!"

Pray: Almighty God, whose compassion never fails and who invites us to call upon You in prayer, hear the heartfelt confession of our sins and receive our humble supplication for Your mercy. Spare us from the just punishment of sin, which our Lord Jesus Christ has borne for us, and enable us to serve You in holiness and purity of life; through Jesus Christ, our Lord, who lives and reigns with You and the Holy Spirit, one God, now and forever. Amen. (Collect from Day of Supplication and Prayer, *Altar Book*)

Lesson 2

The Lord's Judgment of Nineveh

The Lord's swift judgment of Nineveh brings deliverance to His people. Nineveh, representative of the Assyrian Empire, once a hammer and instrument of the Lord's wrath against the wicked, has now become the object of His wrath. Nineveh, who became rich on the spoils of war, was about to be looted. Nahum is prophesying about the restoration of Israel.

Destruction and Restoration

Read Nahum 2:1–2. In many ways, the Assyrian Empire (Nineveh) was wicked and evil. Yet the Lord used Assyria as His instrument.

11. Read Jeremiah 25:9; 51:20–23. Babylon is called the Lord's servant. How can the Lord use evil, like Assyria and Babylon, for good?

12. Read Psalm 80:8–13 and Ephesians 5:27. How was the majesty of Jacob and Israel ultimately restored?

Nineveh Pillaged

Read Nahum 2:3–10. Verses 3–4 mention soldiers clothed in red (scarlet or vermilion). Ezekiel 23:14–15 mentions that these soldiers clothed in red are the Babylonians (Chaldeans). Nahum prophesies that the Babylonians will destroy or punish the Assyrians. Martin Luther in commenting on Psalm 110:3 writes, "They deserve nothing better than that God should punish one rogue by another" (AE 13:274).

13. How does the Lord use evil to punish evil?

In verse 5, Nahum speaks of the King of Assyria, who sees his officers and army stumbling around. Martin Luther writes, "So great is their loss of hope, so great is their shock, that they do not even dare to go outside the city to face the Chaldeans" (AE 18:302). Ultimately, the Assyrians have no hope, because the Lord is against them.

14. Read Ephesians 1:18; 2:12. What does it mean for a Christian to have hope?

Read Isaiah 22:8. The Lord often speaks of being stripped as a punishment. To be stripped by one's enemy is shameful. Today, some people say that in general people no longer know the difference between right and wrong but do recognize or are affected by shame.

15. Discuss recent events where famous people were shamed. How is shame an indicator of sin, wrong, or punishment?

The Lion's Den Taunt

Read Nahum 2:11–13. Lions are known as the king of the jungle. They have sole rule (monarchy) because other animals do not challenge them. The Assyrian Empire, with Nineveh as its capital, had sole rule of the Middle East during Nahum's time.

16. Read Isaiah 5:29 and Jeremiah 2:15. The Assyrian kings liked to fancy themselves as lions. Here Nahum, under the inspiration of the Holy Spirit, taunts and mocks Assyria by asking, "Where is the lions' den?" What do you think of the prophet mocking the Lord's enemy?

The Scriptures often compare the wicked to lions. Proverbs 28:15 compares wicked rulers to roaring lions. In 1 Peter 5:8, Satan is compared to a roaring lion. Lions are predators that few animals can escape.

17. How is the image of a roaring lion fitting as an enemy of the Lord's people?

18. Read Ezekiel 13:8. What does it mean when the Lord is against you?

God's Word for Today

One observation we can make from this section of Nahum is how the Lord works through means. In this particular chapter, rather than send fire from heaven to consume Nineveh, the Lord uses another wicked nation to destroy the Assyrian Empire. As Martin Luther described it, "God should punish one rogue by another." The Lord uses nations, people, and even the devil for His purposes. The Lord indeed is the Lord of history. In fact, the Lord ultimately uses history for the salvation of His chosen people and the deliverance of His Church.

19. Read Romans 13:1–7. How does the Lord use government (even a wicked government) for the purpose of judgment?

20. Read Matthew 25:31–40. How does the Lord use Christians in particular as His instruments of mercy?

In Closing

Encourage participants to begin the following activities:

- Read, listen to, or watch the news. Consider how the Lord uses world events for His purposes.
- Pray that the Lord thwart evil in the world.
- Read Nahum 3 to prepare for the next section.

Sing or read together "Rise! To Arms! With Prayer Employ You" (*LSB* 668):

1. Rise! To arms! With prayer employ you,
O Christians, lest the foe destroy you;
For Satan has designed your fall.
Wield God's Word, the weapon glorious;
Against all foes be thus victorious,
For God protects you from them all.
Fear not the hordes of hell,
Here is Emmanuel. Hail the Savior!
The strong foes yield To Christ, our shield,
And we, the victors, hold the field.

2. Cast afar this world's vain pleasure
And boldly strive for heav'nly treasure.
Be steadfast in the Savior's might.
Trust the Lord, who stands beside you,
For Jesus from all harm will hide you.

By faith you conquer in the fight.
Take courage, weary soul!
Look forward to the goal!
Joy awaits you. The race well run,
Your long war won,
Your crown shines splendid as the sun.

3. Wisely fight, for time is fleeting;
The hours of grace are fast retreating;
Short, short is this our earthly way.
When the Lord the dead will waken
And sinners all by fear are shaken,
The saints with joy will greet that day.
Praise God, our triumph's sure.
We need not long endure Scorn and trial.
Our Savior King His own will bring
To that great glory which we sing.

Pray: O God, the protector of all who trust in You, without whom nothing is strong and nothing is holy, multiply Your mercy on us that, with You as our ruler and guide, we may so pass through things temporal that we lose not the things eternal; through Jesus Christ, our Lord, who lives and reigns with You and the Holy Spirit, one God, now and forever. Amen. (Third Sunday after Trinity, *Altar Book*)

Lesson 3

Woe over Nineveh

As if the depiction of Nineveh's destruction in the first two chapters was not enough, Nahum continues to vividly describe her devastation. The very horrors of war Nineveh used against other nations will be used against the Assyrian Empire. No one will mourn the destruction of Nineveh. The men, women, and even infants will be destroyed—a people to be remembered no more.

Luther writes, "The prophet is still pressing home his prophecy about the ruin of Nineveh and the destruction of the kingdom of the Assyrians. You see, no matter how much he has mentioned all this in considerable detail earlier in the second chapter, he is still having pleasure and, in the Spirit, uses a profusion of varied expressions and figures. As is the custom of the prophets, he repeats the same ones" (AE 18:306).

21. What is it to be remembered no more?

22. Why do you think that the Lord repeats the same themes using different words?

City of Blood

Read Nahum 3:1–3 and Ezekiel 24:6–9. Assyria was known for shedding the blood of her enemies, of turning the cities she invaded into cities of blood. Now Nineveh would be turned into a city of blood.

The atrocities the Assyrians committed against others would be done to them.

23. Why is it necessary that punishment result in the shedding of blood?

On this section of Nahum, Luther writes, "God's patience is great, as all Scripture repeatedly indicates. He bears our sins with great tolerance so long as they are hidden. When, however, we have become so blind that even the people in the street are aware of them so that our sins seem to become part of us and we make a habit of them, then clearly He can no longer bear them. He notes them and punishes them" (AE 18:306–307).

24. Why do public sins, public evil, or public atrocities use up the Lord's patience more quickly than those done in private?

Comparisons of Nineveh

Read Nahum 3:4–11. In verses 4–7, Nineveh is compared to a prostitute. Once again, Nahum uses the image of exposed nakedness for shame. The Lord uses the image of prostitution (sometimes graphically) to illustrate sin and wickedness against Him.

25. See Ezekiel 16:15–22. How is prostitution a fitting image for sin against God?

In Nahum 3:8–11, Nineveh is compared to Thebes and Cush—two Egyptian cities. These powerful cities were destroyed by the Assyrians in 663 BC. In a similar manner, Nineveh would fall and be destroyed by the Babylonians. In fact, Nineveh's destruction would be so complete that her proud soldiers would be afraid to fight, women and children would be killed, and even infants would be slaughtered horrifically. To many people today, such horrors seem unjust. Yet the Lord brought this upon the Assyrians.

26. How can a gracious God bring such harsh judgment and punishment against His enemies?

Final Taunts

Read Nahum 3:12–19. The final verses of Nahum describe the utter futility of Nineveh's defense. No matter what is tried, it will fail. Nineveh's fortresses will fall like ripe fruit. The prophets often describe the wicked as drunkards.

27. Read Psalm 75:8. How does the Lord give the drunkard his fill?

Nahum tells the Ninevites to multiply like locusts in order to raise up troops to defend the city. Yet, no matter how Nineveh tries to increase its population, the city will be swarmed and devoured. In the Minor Prophets, population decline is seen as a sign of judgment.

28. Why is a decreasing population a judgment from God?

God's **Word for Today**

Luther closes out Nahum with these words: "Here we see how everything in this prophet is filled with the comfort with which God Almighty comforts His godly people against the mighty taunting of the enemy. These consolations ought also to fill us all with courage in any need, so that we may have confidence and trust absolutely that the Lord will not allow foes of God's Word to prevail against us" (AE 18:315).

Luther wrote these words at a critical period during the Reformation. Luther himself was in danger. The scriptural teaching on the Lord's Supper that Christ gives His true body and blood was under attack. From Nahum and the judgment against the Assyrians and the city of Nineveh, Luther draws comfort and courage.

29. Who and what are enemies of the Word of God that cause you to lose courage?

30. How does hearing how the Lord delivered His people from the Assyrians give you comfort today?

In Closing

Encourage participants to begin the following activities:

- Pray for Christians who are afflicted and persecuted throughout the world.
- When you feel discouraged or afflicted, take comfort in how the Lord delivered His people, as described in the Book of Nahum.
- Read Habakkuk 1 to prepare for the next section.

Sing or read together "The Day Is Surely Drawing Near" (*LSB* 508):

1. The day is surely drawing near
When Jesus, God's anointed,
In all His power shall appear
As judge whom God appointed.
Then fright shall banish idle mirth,
And flames on flames shall ravage earth
As Scripture long has warned us.

4. Then woe to those who scorned the Lord
And sought but carnal pleasures,
Who here despised His precious Word
And loved their earthly treasures!
With shame and trembling they will stand
And at the judge's stern command
To Satan be delivered.

7. O Jesus Christ, do not delay,
But hasten our salvation;
We often tremble on our way
In fear and tribulation
O hear and grant our fervent plea:
Come, mighty judge, and set us free
From death and ev'ry evil.

Pray: Lord Jesus Christ, so govern our hearts and minds by Your Holy Spirit that, ever mindful of Your glorious return, we may persevere in both faith and holiness of living; for You live and reign with the Father and the Holy Spirit, one God, forever and ever. Amen. (Collect for the Last Sunday of the Church Year, Series B, *Altar Book*)

Lesson 4

Is the Lord Just?

The first chapter of Habakkuk sets the tone for the rest of the book. Habakkuk first asks how long he must cry out for help, and then he asks why the Lord tolerates evil. These are questions people still ask today. The Lord gives two answers to Habakkuk: look at what I am about to do, and write down My revelation. The Lord's Word addresses both of these questions.

Luther thought Habakkuk's name meant "heartener or comforter." Today most scholars think his name comes from Akkadian and refers to an herb or tree. Other than his name, nothing is known of Habakkuk, although there are some apocryphal stories that he assisted Daniel in the lions' den. Habakkuk is relevant today because he asks the same questions we ask today, "Why?" and "How long, O Lord?"

Habakkuk's First Complaint

Read Habakkuk 1:2–4. Habakkuk complains, "O LORD, how long shall I cry for help, and You will not hear?"

31. What business does Habakkuk or anyone else have complaining to God?

Habakkuk complains that "the law is paralyzed" and "justice goes forth perverted." Martin Luther understands this complaint to be "might before right" (AE 19:163).

32. What are some examples of "might before right"?

The Lord Answers

Read Habakkuk 1:5–11. To Habakkuk's first complaint, the Lord replies, "Look among the nations, and see; wonder and be astounded. For I am doing a work in your days that you would not believe if told."

33. Read Romans 11:33. How has the Lord saved His people throughout history in wonderful and astonishing ways?

34. The Lord ends His reply to Habakkuk in verse 11. The Babylonians who were the Lord's instruments for destroying the Assyrians and chastening the Israelites will be swept away. How did the Babylonians sin?

Habakkuk's Second Complaint

Read Habakkuk 1:12–2:1. Habakkuk pleads with "my Holy One."

35. Read Leviticus 20:8. On what basis can Habakkuk (and we) call the Lord, "my Holy One"?

36. In 1:13, Habakkuk asks the Lord, "Why do You . . . remain silent when the wicked swallows up the man more righteous than he?"

Verse 17 deals with greed and has a plea to the Lord for deliverance. "Is he then to keep on emptying his net?" Conquering one nation makes a man want to conquer another. Greed begets greed; lust begets lust; coveting makes one desire his neighbor's possessions more.

37. Read Proverbs 25:28; 1 Corinthians 7:9; 9:25; and 2 Timothy 2:5. The Scriptures extol self-control. How can Christians exercise self-control?

Habakkuk wrestles with God and in faith holds Him to His promises.

38. See Genesis 18:23–32 and 2 Corinthians 12:7–10. How is wrestling with God or holding Him to His promises an act of faith?

God's Word for Today

Oftentimes it is difficult to understand why the Lord allows evil to continue in this world or why it seems as if He is not punishing the wicked. Yet when the Christian is in need, he or she clings to the promises of God all the more. Luther writes, "Thereby God shows us clearly that He does not want us to rely on anything at all except solely on His grace and mercy. . . . And God cannot tolerate that anyone relies on anything but on His grace. He destroys any other object of reliance together with all who rely on it. However, flesh and blood cannot believe this. This seems much too strange to them" (AE 19:166).

39. Read Acts 13:40–41. How does St. Paul apply Habakkuk 1:5 to Christ?

Habakkuk has witnessed much evil. He sees that the Babylonians are about to conquer the Lord's people, and he knows the promise of the coming Messiah. By faith, Habakkuk clings to the promises of

God. We also see evil and suffering in the world. We have hardships and trials.

40. How does the life of Christ show us how faith lives among trials and temptations?

In Closing

Encourage participants to begin the following activities:

- Pray for those suffering trials, temptations, and hardships so that their faith may remain strong in the promises of God.
- Trust that the Lord will not allow you to be tempted beyond your ability to bear it, or rather beyond His ability to preserve you.
- Read Habakkuk 2 to prepare for the next section.

Sing or read together "Jesus Christ, My Sure Defense" (*LSB* 741):

1. Jesus Christ, my sure defense
And my Savior, now is living!
Knowing this, my confidence
Rests upon the hope here given,
Though the night of death be fraught
Still with many an anxious thought.

2. Jesus, my Redeemer, lives;
Likewise I to life shall waken.
He will bring me where He is;
Shall my courage then be shaken?
Shall I fear, or could the Head
Rise and leave His members dead?

3. No, too closely I am bound
By my hope to Christ forever;
Faith's strong hand the Rock has found,
Grasped it, and will leave it never;
Even death now cannot part
From its Lord the trusting heart.

Pray: Merciful and everlasting God, You did not spare Your only Son but delivered Him up for us all to bear our sins on the cross. Grant that our hearts may be so fixed with steadfast faith in Him that we fear not the power of sin, death, and the devil; through the same Jesus Christ, our Lord, who lives and reigns with You and the Holy Spirit, one God, now and forever. Amen. (Collect for Wednesday in Holy Week, *Altar Book*)

Lesson 5

The Lord's Justice Is Certain

The Lord's answer to Habakkuk's complaint is that His justice is certain. The Lord does not rebuke Habakkuk for reminding the Lord of His promises; rather, the Lord instructs Habakkuk to write His oracle on tablets so future generations can read them. The vision given by the Lord is to provide comfort, for the Lord is fulfilling His promise. This chapter proclaims the Gospel beautifully and clearly: "the righteous shall live by his faith."

The Righteous Shall Live By Faith

Read Habakkuk 2:2–5. Habakkuk is instructed to write the vision he received on tablets. Prophets often wrote on a scroll or in a book, but Habakkuk was told to write on a tablet. In Exodus 31:18; 32:15–16; and Deuteronomy 27:8, Moses is instructed to write on tablets.

41. What is the significance in Habakkuk being told to use tablets rather than a scroll or a book to record the vision given to him by the Lord?

"The vision awaits its appointed time. . . . it will surely come" (2:3). Habakkuk was confronted with the reality that captivity and destruction were coming to Jerusalem. Yet his hope was in the coming Christ. He believed that the Lord would deliver on His promise. Luther noted that there were three messages inscribed on the tablets: promise, exhortation, and threat.

42. How does this threefold message sustain and preserve faith?

Habakkuk concludes the inscription on the tablet with the words, "the righteous shall live by his faith" (Habakkuk 2:4b).

43. Some have said that the Old Testament is a "works righteous" religion, while the New Testament is based on "faith." What does this passage from Habakkuk indicate about how the Lord provides righteousness?

Woe to the Evildoer

Read Habakkuk 2:6–8. Woe is announced to those who reap what they do not sow. The primary purpose of Habakkuk is to comfort and sustain the faith of those who will witness the destruction of Jerusalem. It is to give people hope regarding the coming of Christ. Habakkuk employs taunts to raise the spirits of the people. The Babylonians have acquired wealth by unjustly taking from others. All the wealth they acquired will be taken from them. Habakkuk says the "remnant" of the people will plunder Babylon. The weak will defeat the bully, so to speak.

44. How does the triumph of the remnant over the strong fit the pattern the Lord uses throughout Scripture?

Read Habakkuk 2:9–11. Woe to the greedy. In verse 11, responding to Babylon's sin, the stones of the walls and the beams of the woodwork cry out. Read Luke 19:40. On Palm Sunday, the Pharisees ask Jesus to silence His followers, and Jesus replies that if they were silenced the "stones would cry out." Babylon's wickedness and greed is so great that even the stones and beams cry out against her.

45. Read Romans 8:19–23. Why does creation itself react against Babylon?

Read Habakkuk 2:12–14. "Woe to him who builds a town with blood" (v. 12). Recall that Nahum pronounced judgment on the Assyrians for building upon bloodshed. Now Habakkuk pronounces judgment against the Babylonians for the same reason. Luther writes, "When kings have too much money, they tend to erect many useless buildings. . . . [the builder] is doing all of this with the sweat and the blood of the poor, with unjust goods, acquired through imposition of taxes and through threats of physical harm. . . . he conquered such great countries and nations with much needless bloodshed and with injustice" (AE 19:215). In this case, the subjection of the Jews to the Babylonians to construct such buildings was persecution of the Lord's people.

46. How does the destruction of the Babylonian Empire fill the earth "with the knowledge of the glory of the LORD"?

Read Habakkuk 2:15–17. Woe to the drunk and violent. In this section, the Lord speaks of the Babylonian Empire as a drunkard. Babylon will drink the wrath of the Lord and, as in Nahum 3:5, will be put to shame. Because of how Babylon has treated the nations, everyone is hoping for her downfall. "They will mock and ridicule you. For everybody is wishing you that fate, and you surely also deserve it" (AE 19:221).

47. How does pride blind a person so that he cannot see the coming judgment?

Read Habakkuk 2:18–20. Woe to the idol maker. This fifth woe against Babylon deals with her worship. The king of Babylon worships his own creation. The prophets of Israel frequently mock idols and those who say "to a silent stone, Arise!" Here Habakkuk proclaims that the Lord dwells in His holy temple and that the world will keep silent before Him. This might remind us of the hymn "Let All Mortal Flesh Keep Silence" (*LSB* 621).

48.Why would a person keep silent in the presence of the holy Lord?

God's Word for Today

In this chapter, despite the judgment that came to Jerusalem, the Lord promised that His justice is certain. This section of Habakkuk emphasizes how the actions of man do not add up to righteousness and that our righteousness comes by faith, faith in Christ Jesus.

49. Read Romans 1:16–17. How is the righteousness of God revealed in faith?

50. Read Genesis 15:6. How is faith the key to understanding righteousness in both the Old and New Testaments?

In Closing

Encourage participants to begin the following activities:

- Remember that our righteousness comes by faith in Christ Jesus, not in actions. This gives us great freedom to do good works for our neighbor.
- Pray for the Church, that the Word of God may be proclaimed boldly and faithfully.
- Read Habakkuk 3 to prepare for the next section.

Sing or read together "The Law of God Is Good and Wise" (*LSB* 579):

1. The Law of God is good and wise
And sets His will before our eyes,
Shows us the way of righteousness,
And dooms to death when we transgress.

2. Its light of holiness imparts
The knowledge of our sinful hearts
That we may see our lost estate
And turn from sin before too late.

3. To those who help in Christ have found
And would in works of love abound
It shows what deeds are His delight
And should be done as good and right.

4. But those who scornfully disdain
God's Law shall then in sin remain;
Its terror in their ear resounds
And keeps their wickedness in bounds.

5. The Law is good; but since the fall
Its holiness condemns us all;
It dooms us for our sin to die
And has no pow'r to justify.

6. To Jesus we for refuge flee,
Who from the curse has set us free,
And humbly worship at His throne,
Saved by His grace through faith alone.

Pray: O God, our refuge and strength, the author of all godliness, by Your grace hear the prayers of Your Church. Grant that those things which we ask in faith we may receive through Your bountiful mercy; through Jesus Christ, Your Son, our Lord, who lives and reigns with You and the Holy Spirit, one God, now and forever. Amen. (Collect Proper 22C, *Altar Book*)

Lesson 6

Habakkuk's Prayer

The third chapter of Habakkuk is a beautiful prayer in the form of a psalm. It is a hymn of praise. This chapter brings Habakkuk to a climactic end. In this chapter, (1) we hear that Israel (the Lord's people and Church) will be saved; (2) the theodicy questions (why the good suffer and the evil prosper) Habakkuk asks are answered in the Lord's judgment and deliverance; and (3) the conclusion of the Lord's work brings joy. Habakkuk rejoices in the Lord.

Bring Us Help

Read Habakkuk 3:1–2. This prayer or psalm takes the pattern of psalms such as 17; 86; 90; 102; and 142. It also contains the odd word *Shigionoth*, which is transliterated from the Hebrew. The meaning of the word is unknown, but most scholars believe it to be a liturgical or musical term. Read the first couple of verses of the psalms mentioned above.

51. How can we learn to pray from the Psalms and from this prayer of Habakkuk?

In chapter 1, Habakkuk "complained" to the Lord regarding the prosperity of the wicked and the plight of the righteous. In chapter 2, the Lord answered. Here in chapter 3, Habakkuk offers thanksgiving and praise for what the Lord has spoken. He calls upon the Lord to make the report of His work known and to remember mercy. On the basis of the Lord's deliverance of His people in the past, Habakkuk wants the Lord to deliver His people once again. Habakkuk says that in tribulation God should remember mercy.

52. When you pray the *kyrie eleison* ("Lord have mercy") in the liturgy, what are you asking the Lord for?

Judgment of Midian

Read Habakkuk 3:3–7. Verse 3 ends with the word *Selah*. Other than here in Habakkuk, the word only occurs in the Psalms. While the meaning of the word is not known, it indicates that this poem of Habakkuk was used in Israel's worship. Specific places such as Mount Paran and Teman are mentioned.

53. What occurred at these places?

Often times we imagine the Lord dwelling in the heavens. Here in Habakkuk 3:3–7, the Lord comes in His glory not from the heavens but from specific, concrete places on earth.

54. Why is it significant that the Lord approaches and displays His glory from the earth rather than the heavens?

Judgment of the Flood

Read Habakkuk 3:8–10. In this section, judgment and salvation are mentioned in connection with water. Luther notes that this section can be understood in a positive or negative manner. Regarding the positive interpretation, Luther writes, "After the prophet has related a few miracles of God, he rejoices in the Lord and speaks lovingly to Him, saying: 'I believe indeed that it was mercy and not anger when You rode in the flood of the sea and its waters on Your horses and on Your chariots, that is, on the horses and chariots of Israel. For You were present and led them through, effecting complete salvation and victory. There no trace of wrath or anger that You might have entertained could be detected'" (AE 19:232).

55. How can the Lord's judgment for one group be mercy for another?

This section also speaks of the mountains trembling, which calls to mind passages like Exodus 19:18 and Judges 5:5. It speaks of disturbances on the sea and the land because of the Lord's presence. These sorts of natural disaster events call to mind the signs of the end times. See Matthew 24:29–31.

56. How do natural disasters, such as earthquakes and storms, reflect both the Lord's judgment on the earth and His salvation for His people?

Judgment against Egypt

Read Habakkuk 3:11–15. The "sun and moon" standing in their place is a reference to the long day in Joshua 10:12–13. Note that in Joshua 10:14 it says, "The LORD fought for Israel."

57. In this section of Habakkuk, who is the subject of the verbs, that is, who is doing the action?

58. What comfort does Israel (the Church) have when her enemies appear to be stronger than she?

God's Word for Today

The Lord delivers His people from great adversity and hardship throughout Scripture. The more hopeless the situation, the more faith clings to the promises of God. The Lord's people have the promise that He will work all things for good. When bad things happen, the Christian in faith believes that the Lord will demonstrate an even greater blessing in His deliverance. This certainly was Jesus' view as He died on the cross. Psalm 22 is His prayer. While abandoned by His Father because of our sin—"My God, My God, why have You forsaken Me?"—He clung to the promises of God and believed. Psalm 22:19–31 is Christ's prayer of faith that hopes in the deliverance of His Father. Indeed, Jesus rose from the dead. Christ's prayer becomes our prayer.

Read Habakkuk 3:17–19.

59. Note Habakkuk 3:18. See Psalms 9:14; 13:5; 21:1; 35:9; and Luke 1:47. How do the Lord's people have joy in the midst of suffering, trials, and hardship?

60. Read Hebrews 12:2. What "joy" did Jesus have set before Him that He endured the cross?

In Closing

Encourage participants to begin the following activities:

- Recognize that great challenges, sorrows, or troubles in our lives demonstrate how much more the Lord will save and deliver us.
- Take joy in the promises of God and in the gifts He has given you in your life.
- Read Zephaniah 1 to prepare for the next section.

Sing or read together "Song of Habakkuk" (*LSB* 986):

986 Song of Habakkuk

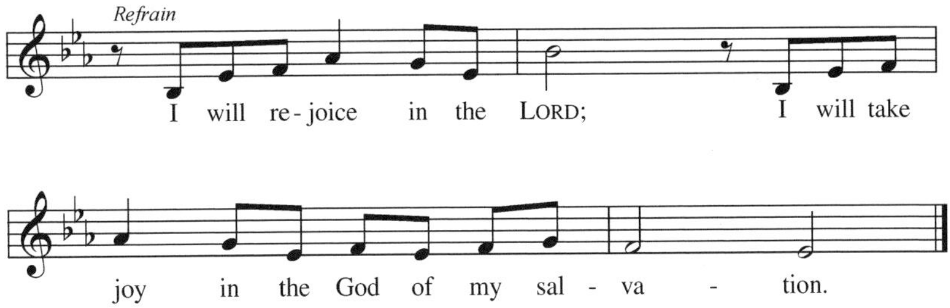

1 O LORD, I have heard the re- | port of You,*
and Your work, O LORD, | do I fear.

2 In the midst of the years revive it; in the midst of the years | make it known;*
in wrath remember | mercy. REFRAIN

3 God came from | Teman,*
and the Holy One from Mount | Paran.

4 His splendor covered the | heavens,*
and the earth was full | of His praise.

5 His brightness was like the light; rays flashed | from His hand;*
and there He | veiled His power.

6 Before Him went | pestilence,*
and plague followed | at His heels.

7 He stood and mea- | sured the earth;*
He looked and shook the | nations;

8 then the eternal mountains were scattered; the everlasting hills | sank low.*
His were the ever- | lasting ways. REFRAIN

9 You went out for the salvation of Your | people,*
for the salvation of Your a- | nointed.

10 You crushed the head of the house of the | wicked,*
laying him bare from | thigh to neck.

11 Yet I will rejoice | in the LORD;*
I will take joy in the God of my sal- | vation.

12 GOD, the Lord, is my strength; He makes my feet | like the deer's;*
He makes me tread on my high | places.

gp Glory be to the Father and | to the Son*
and to the Holy | Spirit;
as it was in the be- | ginning,*
is now, and will be forever. | Amen. REFRAIN

Pray: O God, the strength of all who put their trust in You, mercifully grant that by Your power we may be defended against all adversity; through Jesus Christ, Your Son, our Lord, who lives and reigns with You and the Holy Spirit, one God, now and forever. Amen. (Collect Epiphany 7C, *Altar Book*)

Lesson 7

The Lord Judges Judah

Zephaniah prophesied during the time of Jeremiah and, like Jeremiah, was told to preserve his prophecy for future generations. His name means "he whom Yahweh hides" or "hidden of Yahweh." Unlike other prophets, some of whom provide very little information about their genealogy, Zephaniah's lineage goes back four generations to King Hezekiah, a good king of Judah. In a sense, Zephaniah is going back to the Church of his grandfather. He preaches about the coming "day of the Lord" when sin would be punished and the faithful remnant of the Lord would be saved.

Zephaniah 1:1 is the inscription for the book. Instead of appearing to the people like He did at Mount Sinai, the Lord hides His glory and speaks through the prophet.

61. Read Deuteronomy 18:15–17. How does Zephaniah fulfill what is spoken of in Deuteronomy 18?

62. How are pastors today a fulfillment of Deuteronomy 18?

The Coming Judgment

Read Zephaniah 1:2. Zephaniah begins with a startling and alarming pronouncement that everything will be swept off the face of the earth. This is total destruction.

63. Read Genesis 6:5–7. How is the destruction threatened in Zephaniah similar to that of the flood?

64. Read Zephaniah 1:3. Notice that the list given here—man and beast, birds, fish—is the exact opposite of the order of creation in Genesis 1–2, where man is the last creature created by God. Why does the Lord's judgment against man also affect the rest of creation?

65. Read Zephaniah 1:4–6. What sin or offense is causing the Lord to execute His wrath and judgment?

The Day of the Lord Is Near

Zephaniah preached during the reign of Josiah, the last good king of Judah. Josiah initiated reforms during his reign (2 Kings 22–23). He repaired the temple, and a Book of the Law that had been lost was found (2 Kings 22:8–20). The ultimate judgment of the Lord is the loss of His Holy Word (through which He is present with His people). Israel/Judah had lost a Book of the Law and received the judgment of God. During Josiah's reforms, the lost book was found, which was the Lord showing His grace and mercy to His people. While it is not possible to determine for certain if Zephaniah prophesied before or after Josiah's reforms, there is good reason to think he prophesied after the lost Book of the Law had been found, due to the many parallels between Zephaniah chapters 1 and 3 and the Book of Deuteronomy. The parallels between Zephaniah 1 and Deuteronomy are listed below.

Zephaniah 1	Deuteronomy
Zeph. 1:13—"Though they build houses, they shall not inhabit them"	Deut. 28:30—"You shall build a house, but you shall not dwell in it."
Zeph. 1:13—"though they plant vineyards, they shall not drink wine from them."	Deut. 28:39—"You shall plant vineyards and dress them, but you shall neither drink of the wine nor gather the grapes."
Zeph. 1:15—"A day of distress and anguish"	Deut. 28:53—"in the siege and in the distress with which your enemies shall distress you."
Zeph. 1:15—"a day of darkness and gloom, a day of clouds and thick darkness"	Deut. 4:11—"wrapped in darkness, cloud, and gloom"
Zeph. 1:17—"I will bring distress on mankind, so that they shall walk like the blind"	Deut. 28:28–29—"The LORD will strike you with madness and blindness and confusion of mind, and you shall grope at noonday, as the blind grope in darkness."
Zeph. 1:18—"In the fire of His jealousy, all the earth shall be consumed."	Deut. 32:21–22—"They have made me jealous. . . . a fire is kindled by my anger. . . . devours the earth and its increase"

In verse 7, Zephaniah announces that the "day of the LORD is near." The "day of the LORD" is a day of the Lord's visitation either for wrath or for mercy. Most often the "day of the LORD" refers to His judgment. In the context of Zephaniah, it is a day of judgment. The wrath of God was to be poured out on Judah. The Babylonians would destroy Jerusalem. Revelation 6:16–17 also describes "the great day of their wrath." The Day of the Lord can arrive at any time.

66. How should Christians prepare for "the day of the LORD"?

67. Zephaniah 1:13–18 harkens back to Deuteronomy, as shown in the chart above. Zephaniah did not invent a new message. Observing

Zephaniah's preaching method and his use of Deuteronomy, what can we learn about preaching in the Church today?

Zephaniah 1:14 says that the "day of the LORD" is "near and hastening fast." Read 2 Peter 3:9–10. Peter teaches that the Lord's patience is greater than man's and that the Lord is patient so that more might hear the Gospel.

68. How can the "day of the LORD" be both "hastening fast" and slow because of the Lord's patience?

God's Word for Today

Zephaniah's referencing of Deuteronomy teaches us about both the Law and the Gospel—about repentance and forgiveness. The lost Book of the Law (Deuteronomy) being found during the reign of Josiah was God's gracious act of restoring His Word to His people. Zephaniah builds on this by echoing the words of Deuteronomy and calling the people to repentance. He preached the curses that Deuteronomy threatened. He also preached the coming judgment against Judah and the final judgment on the Last Day. When Zephaniah preached the Gospel, he recalled the salvific acts of the Lord—how the Lord saved His people in times past—and he called on the Lord to save His people now in a similar way.

When John the Baptist came on the scene, he preached, "Repent, for the kingdom of heaven is at hand." Likewise, Jesus also preached repentance. Every reformation, restoration, and revitalization of the Church of God has begun with the message of repentance. When Martin Luther posted the Ninety-five Theses in 1517, his first thesis said, "When our Lord and Master Jesus Christ said, 'Repent,' He willed the entire life of believers to be one of repentance" (AE 31:25). Repentance and forgiveness is the only way the Church is reformed or revitalized, for it is the Word of God that makes dead and alive.

69. How can the coming of the kingdom of God be understood as a Law (judgment) event and as a Gospel (mercy) event?

70. Why does reformation, renewal, and revitalization of the Church always involve going back to what has been proclaimed forever?

In Closing

Encourage participants to begin the following activities:

- Repent. When you hear about high-profile people or celebrities falling into a scandal or sin, repent of your own sins. When you hear of a natural disaster and a people suffering from it, repent because such a disaster could befall you. Repent, for the Day of the Lord is hastening quickly.
- Take comfort in how the Lord has delivered His people in ages past, having the certainty that the Lord will be faithful to His promise because His Son, Jesus, has taken the punishment for all our sins. Be at peace, for your Lord is coming quickly to save you.
- Read Zephaniah 2 to prepare for the next section.

Sing or read together "All Mankind Fell in Adam's Fall" (*LSB* 562):

1. All mankind fell in Adam's fall;
One common sin infects us all.
From one to all the curse descends,
And over all God's wrath impends.

2. Through all our pow'rs corruption creeps
And us in dreadful bondage keeps;
In guilt we draw our infant breath
And reap its fruits of woe and death.

3. From hearts depraved, to evil prone,
Flow thoughts and deeds of sin alone;
God's image lost, the darkened soul
Seeks not nor finds its heav'nly goal.

4. But Christ, the second Adam, came
To bear our sin and woe and shame,
To be our life, our light, our way,
Our only hope, our only stay.

5. As by one man all mankind fell
And, born in sin, was doomed to hell,
So by one Man, who took our place,
We all were justified by grace.

6. We thank you, Christ; new life is ours,
New light, new hope, new strength, new pow'rs.
This grace our ev'ry way attend
Until we reach our journey's end.

Pray: Almighty and ever-living God, You have given exceedingly great and precious promises to those who trust in You. Dispel from us the works of darkness and grant us to live in the light of Your Son, Jesus Christ, that our faith may never be found wanting; through the same Jesus Christ, our Lord, who lives and reigns with You and the Holy Spirit, one God, now and forever. Amen. (Collect Proper 28A, *Altar Book*)

Lesson 8

The Lord Judges the Nations

Zephaniah chapter 2 has a slightly different perspective than chapter 1. In the first chapter, the style was declaratory and directed at Judah to warn them of the impending Babylonian captivity. In the second chapter, the style is an admonition calling for repentance. The focus is the Gentile nations around Judah—Repent or be destroyed. The first chapter focused on idolatry as the primary offense against the Lord. The second chapter condemns syncretism, that is, the mixing of truth and error by taking elements from various religions. Judgment begins in the house of God and continues to the surrounding nations.

Read Zephaniah 2:1–3. The Lord begins by addressing the "shameless nation." Read Jeremiah 6:15. An indicator of deep perversity in sin is the lack of shame for wrongdoing. The shameless are proud and lack humility, especially before the Lord God.

71. Think of our nation today. Collectively and individually, how are we a "shameless nation"?

In Zephaniah 2:2, the "day of the anger of the LORD" is coming fast. In verse 3, the Lord calls out for the "humble of the land" to "Seek the LORD. . . . seek righteousness; seek humility."

72. How do you seek the Lord and His righteousness and humility?

Judgment upon the Nations

Read Zephaniah 2:4–7. Judgment to the west (Philistia). In Nahum 2:13, the Lord said, "I am against you." Here in Zephaniah, the Lord turns against Philistia and promises to give this land to the remnant of Judah. Judgment against Judah's enemies is Gospel for the Lord's people. Judah did go into captivity in Babylon, but after seventy years the Lord restored them.

73. Read Luke 1:68. How is this a fulfillment of the Lord's promise to "be mindful of them"?

Read Zephaniah 2:8–11. Judgment to the east (Moab and Ammon). In verse 8, the Lord reports that He heard of great sins from the Moabites and the Ammonites. The Ammonites were a race born out of incest (see Genesis 19:30–38). Amos 1:13 reports that the Ammonites rip open pregnant women. The Lord roots His curse in His own life; "as I live," this judgment will come upon Moab and Ammon. There is no escape, for the Moabites and Ammonites have made themselves enemies of God by being enemies of His chosen people. Yet in the destruction of the Moabites and Ammonites, the Lord will restore His people and establish His kingdom.

74. In Zephaniah 2:11, how does the Lord show His glory to "all the lands of the nations"?

75. Verse 10 notes that the sin that overthrew Moab and Ammon is pride. See Isaiah 16:6 and Jeremiah 48:29. How is pride the root of many (all) sins?

76. Read Zephaniah 2:12. Judgment to the south (Cush). Cush is Judah's enemy to the south (Egypt). Why is the cup of wrath coming to Cush?

Read Zephaniah 2:13–15. Judgment to the north (Assyria). In verses 13–14, there is a reversal of the created order. Man's dominion over creation is taken away. Nineveh becomes a desert wasteland. The beasts of the wild overtake it. Xenophon, the Greek historian, reports in 401 BC that Nineveh could not be found in the sands of the desert. Quite literally, the greatest city in the world was overthrown by the Lord.

77. How is the loss of dominion over creation a punishment from the Lord?

In verse 15, the text reads, "Everyone who passes by her hisses and shakes his fist." This echoes Nahum 3:19, which says that people rejoice and clap their hands to hear of Nineveh's destruction.

78. Can a righteous person "rejoice" at the destruction of evil?

God's Word for Today

This chapter shows us that the Lord, while starting with the household of faith, also extends His judgment to the nations. Every nation surrounding Judah ended up judged. They were judged for being enemies of the Lord's people, that is, pridefully challenging the Lord over whom He should choose to be His people, and for idolatry.

79. Read 1 Peter 4:17–19. How did judgment begin with Jesus, the Son of God?

80. What does it mean for the suffering to entrust their souls to a faithful Creator?

In Closing

Encourage participants to begin the following activities:

- Seek the Lord while He may be found in His Word and Sacraments.
- Pray for repentance beginning in the household of faith and extending out into the world: west, east, south, and north.
- Read Zephaniah 3 to prepare for the next section.

Sing or read together "When All the World Was Cursed" (*LSB* 346):

1. When all the world was cursed
By Moses' condemnation,
Saint John the Baptist came
With words of consolation.
With true forerunner's zeal
The greater One he named,
And Him, as yet unknown,
As Savior he proclaimed.

2. Before he yet was born,
He leaped in joyful meeting,
Confessing Him as Lord
Whose mother he was greeting.
By Jordan's rolling stream,
A new Elijah bold,
He testified of Him
Of whom the prophets told:

3. Behold the Lamb of God
That bears the world's transgression,
Whose sacrifice removes

The devil's dread oppression.
Behold the Lamb of God,
Who takes away our sin,
Who for our peace and joy
Will full atonement win.

4. O grant, dear Lord of love,
That we receive, rejoicing,
The word proclaimed by John,
Our true repentance voicing,
That gladly we may walk
Upon our Savior's way
Until we live with Him
In His eternal day.

Pray: O Lord, graciously hear the prayers of Your people that we who justly suffer the consequence of our sin may be mercifully delivered by Your goodness to the glory of Your name; through Jesus Christ, Your Son, our Lord, who lives and reigns with You and the Holy Spirit, one God, now and forever. Amen. (Sixth Sunday after the Epiphany, Series B, *Altar Book*)

Lesson 9

The Day of the Lord Is Restoration

After describing the desolation that would come to the nations surrounding Judah, the Lord directs His focus to the city of Jerusalem. When the Babylonians came, the city of Jerusalem was destroyed. Christ Jesus in Matthew 24:2 says, “There will not be left here one stone upon another.” He described the destruction of Jerusalem for rejecting Him as the Messiah. Yet out of this, the Lord promises to restore His people. First, He brought His people back from the Babylonian captivity. Now He has restored His people through the Church in Christ Jesus. On the Day of the Lord, Jesus will call and gather His people to be with Him forever.

“We have the clear and abundant Word of God. It brings light to many. The rest, however, despise and persecute it. For these the wrath of God remains. After all, it is impossible for the Lord not to avenge the contempt of His Word. Accordingly, we can declare with the greatest certainty that a terrible evil will come upon those who despise the Word. You see, we cannot be deceived in this point. Furthermore, even when the sincere Word is restored, those will never be lacking who are going to corrupt the Word and that pure wine until Christ comes and puts an end to this evil and destroys them all” (AE 18:349).

81. Read Zephaniah 3:1–2. Of what sin is the “city” (Jerusalem) guilty?

82. The city is defiled or polluted. Read Ezra 2:62; Nehemiah 7:64; and Numbers 35:32–33. What made the city polluted?

Back to Deuteronomy

As in Zephaniah chapter 1, chapter 3 has a few allusions or references back to Deuteronomy.

Zephaniah 3	**Deuteronomy**
Zeph. 3:5—"The LORD within her is righteous; He does no injustice"	Deut. 32:4—" . . . for all His ways are justice. A God of faithfulness and without iniquity, just and upright is He."
Zeph. 3:17—"He will rejoice over you with gladness"	Deut. 28:63—"And as the LORD took delight in doing you good and multiplying you, so the LORD will take delight in bringing ruin upon you and destroying you." Deut. 30:9—"For the LORD will again take delight in prospering you, as He took delight in your fathers."
Zeph. 3:20—"for I will make you renowned and praised among all the peoples of the earth"	Deut. 26:19—"and that He will set you in praise and in fame and in honor high above all nations that He has made, and that you shall be a people holy to the LORD your God, as He promised."

83. What does it mean that the "LORD within her is righteous"?

84. What is it for the Lord to rejoice or delight in you?

85. How does the Lord make us renowned and praised?

The Remnant and the Nations Purified

86. Read Zephaniah 3:9–13. What is the pure speech the Lord puts on their lips?

87. Who are the worshipers from beyond the rivers of Cush?

88. Read Matthew 5:3. What is the blessing of a humble and lowly people?

God's Word for Today

Read Zephaniah 3:14–20. Zephaniah began with the complete and utter destruction of the cosmos because of God's wrath. The book ends with Israel restored. The Lord has a people for Himself. The judgments have been taken away, because Christ has borne the punishment on the cross. The Lord is in the midst of His people, strong and mighty to save them. We no longer have to fear evil. The Lord rejoices with His people. The Lord rejoices in His people.

89. Read Zephaniah 3:15. Why do we never have to fear evil again?

90. Read Luke 10:21 and Hebrews 12:2. What is it for Christ to rejoice in His people?

In Closing

Encourage participants to begin the following activities:

- Rejoice in the salvation the Lord has given you.
- Pray that the Lord's kingdom increase by praying for the Lord of the harvest to send workers into His field.

Sing or read together "Hark! A Thrilling Voice Is Sounding" (*LSB* 345):

1. Hark! A thrilling voice is sounding!
"Christ is near," we hear it say.
"Cast away the works of darkness,
All you children of the day!"

2. Startled at the solemn warning,
Let the earthbound soul arise;
Christ, its sun, all sloth dispelling,
Shines upon the morning skies.

3. See, the Lamb, so long expected,
Comes with pardon down from heav'n.
Let us haste, with tears of sorrow,
One and all, to be forgiv'n;

4. So, when next He comes in glory
And the world is wrapped in fear,
He will shield us with His mercy
And with words of love draw near.

5. Honor, glory, might, dominion
To the Father and the Son
With the ever-living Spirit
While eternal ages run!

Pray: Lord Jesus Christ, we implore You to hear our prayers and to lighten the darkness of our hearts by Your gracious visitation; for You live and reign with the Father and Holy Spirit, one God, now and forever. Amen. (Collect Advent 3C, *Altar Book*)

Leader Notes

These notes are provided as a safety net, a place to turn for help in answering questions and for enriching discussion. They will not answer every question raised in your class. Please read them along with the questions before class. Consult them in class only after exploring the Bible references and discussing what they teach. Please note the different abilities of your class members. Some will easily find the Bible passages listed in this study; others will struggle. To make participation easier, team up members of the class. For example, if a question requires people to look up several passages, assign one passage to one group, the second to another, and so on. Divide the work. Let participants present the answers they discover.

Preparing to Teach Nahum, Habakkuk, Zephaniah

To prepare to lead this study, read through the Books of Nahum, Habakkuk, and Zephaniah. You might read the introductions to them in *The Lutheran Study Bible* or a Bible handbook. Maps of the ancient Middle East at about 700–600 BC would also be of great help.

If you have the opportunity, you will find it helpful to make use of other biblical reference works in the course of your study. These commentaries can be very helpful: James J. Westendorf, *Nahum/Habakkuk/Zephaniah*, People's Bible Commentary (Milwaukee: Northwestern Publishing House, 2000; reprinted by Concordia Publishing House, 2005 [revised edition]); and David W. Baker, *Nahum, Habakkuk, Zephaniah: An Introduction and Commentary*, Tyndale Old Testament Commentaries (Downers Grove, Illinois: Inter-Varsity Press, 1988). Although it is not strictly a commentary, the sections on Nahum, Habakkuk, and Zephaniah in *The Word Becoming Flesh* by Horace Hummel (St. Louis: Concordia Publishing House, 1970) also contain valuable material for the proper interpretation of these biblical books.

Group Bible Study

Group Bible study means mutual learning from one another under the guidance of a leader. The Bible is an inexhaustible resource. No one person can discover all it has to offer. The leader should resist the temptation to give answers and so act as an authority. This teaching approach stifles participation by individual members and can actually hamper learning. As a general rule, don't give interpretation, but try to develop interpreters. In other words, don't explain what the learners can discover by themselves. This is not to say that the leader shouldn't share insights and information gained by his or her class members during the lesson, engage them in meaningful sharing and discussion, or lead them to a summary of the lesson at the close.

Have a chalkboard and chalk or newsprint and marker available to emphasize significant points of the lesson. Rephrase your inquiries or the inquiries of participants as questions, problems, or issues. This provokes thought. Keep discussion to the point. List the answers given on the chalkboard or newsprint, then determine the most vital points made in the discussion. Ask additional questions to fill gaps.

The aim of every Bible study is to help people grow spiritually, not merely in biblical and theological knowledge, but in Christian thinking and living. This means growth in Christian attitudes, insights, and skills. The focus of this course must be Christ and the world of our day. The guiding question will be this: What does the Lord teach us about Himself and our life today through Nahum, Habakkuk, and Zephaniah?

Teaching the Old Testament

Teaching the Old Testament can degenerate into mere moralizing in which do-goodism becomes a substitute for the Gospel and sanctification gets confused with justification. Actually, the justified sinner is not moved by Law but by God's grace in Christ to a totally new life. His or her faith in Christ is always at work in every context of life. Meaningful personal Christianity consists of faith flowing from God's grace in Christ and is evidenced in love for other people. Having experienced God's free grace and forgiveness through the merits of Jesus, the Christian daily works in his or her world to reflect the will of God for humanity in every area of human endeavor.

Christian leaders are Gospel-oriented, not Law-oriented. They distinguish between the two. Both Law and Gospel are necessary because the Gospel will mean nothing unless we first have been crushed by the Law and see our sinfulness. There is no genuine Christianity where faith is not followed by lives pleasing to God. In fact, genuine faith is inseparable from life. The Gospel alone gives us the new heart that causes us to love God and our neighbor.

When Christians teach the Old Testament, they do not teach it as Law, but instead as books containing both Law and Gospel. They see the God of the Old Testament as a God of grace, who out of love establishes a covenant of love with His people (Deuteronomy 7:6–9) and forgives their sins. Christians interpret the Old Testament using the New Testament message of fulfilled prophecy through Jesus Christ. They teach as leaders who personally know the Lord Jesus as Savior, the victorious Christ who gives all believers a new life (2 Corinthians 5:17) and a new mission (John 20:21).

Pace Your Teaching

The lessons in this course of study are designed for a study session of at least an hour in length. If it is the desire and intent of the class to complete an entire lesson each session, it will be necessary for you to summarize the content of certain answers or biblical references in order to preserve time. Asking various class members to look up different Bible passages and to read them aloud to the rest of the class will save time over having every class member look up each reference.

Also, you may not want to cover every question in each lesson. This may lead to undue haste and frustration. Be selective. Pace your teaching. Spend no more than five to ten minutes opening the lesson. During the lesson, get the sweep of meaning. Stop occasionally to help the class gain understanding of a word or concept. Allow approximately five minutes for closing the lesson and announcements.

Should your group have more than a one-hour class period, you can be more leisurely, but do not allow any lesson to drag and become tiresome. Keep it moving. Keep it alive. Keep it meaningful. Eliminate some questions, and restrict yourself to those questions that are most meaningful to the members of the class. If most members study the text at home, they can report their findings, and the time gained can be applied to relating the lesson to life.

Good Preparation

Good preparation by you, the leader, usually affects the pleasure and satisfaction the class will experience.

Suggestions to the Leader for Using the Study Guide

This set of lessons is designed to aid Bible study, that is, to aid a consideration of the written Word of God, with discussion and personal application growing out of the text at hand.

The typical lesson is divided into these sections:

1. Theme Verse
2. Objectives
3. Questions and Answers
4. Closing

The theme verse and objectives give you assistance in arousing the interest of the group in the concepts of the lesson. Here is where you stimulate the minds of the class members. Do not linger too long over the introductory remarks.

The questions and answers provide the real spadework necessary for Bible study. Here the class digs, uncovers, and discovers; it gets the facts and observes them. Your comments are needed only to the extent that they help the group understand the text. The questions in this guide, corresponding to sections within the text, are intended to help the participants discover the meaning of the text.

Having determined what the text says, the class is ready to apply the message. Having heard, read, marked, and learned the Word of God, proceed to digest it inwardly through discussion, evaluation, and application. This is done, as this guide suggests, by taking the truths found in Scripture and applying them to the world and Christianity in general and then to personal Christian life. Class time may not permit discussion of all questions and topics. In preparation, you may need to select one or two and focus on them. Close the session by reviewing one important truth from the lesson.

Remember, the Word of God is sacred, but this study guide is not. The notes in this section offer only guidelines and suggestions. Do not hesitate to alter the guidelines or substitute others to meet your needs and the needs of the participants. Adapt your teaching plan to your class and your class period. Good teaching directs the learner to discover for himself or herself. For you, the teacher, this means directing the learner, not giving the learner answers. Choose the verses that should be looked up in Scripture. What discussion questions will you ask and at what points? Write them in the margin of your study guide. Involve class members, but give them clear directions. What practical actions might you propose for the week following the lesson? Which of the items do you consider most important for your class?

Consider how you can best use your teaching period. Do you have forty-five minutes? an hour? or an hour and a half? If time is short, what should you cut? Learn to become a wise steward of class time.

Plan a brief opening devotion using members of the class. Also, be sure to take time to summarize the lesson or have a class member do so.

Remember to pray frequently for yourself and your class. May God the Holy Spirit bless your study and your leading of others into the comforting truths of God's Christ-centered Word.

Lesson 1

The Divine Warrior

Theme verse: *"Behold upon the mountains, the feet of him who brings goods news, who publishes peace!"*

Nahum 1:15

Objectives

By the power of the Holy Spirit working through God's Word, we will:

- learn that the Lord uses suffering and hardship to drive us to His promises.
- be strengthened in faith that the Lord delivers His people from His enemies.
- believe that Nahum was a historical figure who prophesied about Christ.

1. Judgment and adversity are not necessarily one and the same. Judgment is the working of the Law. When a person faces judgment or the working of the Law, he or she might despair of all hope. He or she might become hardened. Or he or she might repent. This is why the Lord's Word proclaims both Law and Gospel. The Law brings us to repentance. The Gospel proclaims that Christ has answered for our sins. In Nahum, the Lord's people were facing hardship. The Assyrians were threatening the land of Judah, just as they had threatened Israel during Jonah's time. The land of Judah seemed to be under judgment, and the people cried to the Lord.

Christ Jesus has answered for the wrath of God for the sins of the world. When we hear of adversity or disaster in the world, we should repent, because we know that because of our sins we deserve punishment. At the same time, we take comfort in the cross of Jesus, where our sins were answered for. The love that Christ shows us then compels us to help our neighbor in need.

2. When every human effort fails, there is nothing else to rely on except the Lord God. God uses trials and suffering (the failure of human efforts) in our lives to drive us to trust in His promises for deliverance. For example, the Lord prevented Abraham and Sarah from having a child until she was physically too old to conceive. Every human effort failed, yet the Lord demonstrated that He would be faithful to His promise. He gave them a son.

When things are going well in our lives, we often forget the Lord. We credit ourselves or our good fortune rather than thank the Lord for His blessings. When trouble comes to us, we see that our human strength has failed us and we turn to the Lord for deliverance. In this way, the Lord uses suffering, trials, and hardship to drive us to seek Him and His help and to trust in Him for every good thing.

3. Nahum 1:1 and Isaiah 13:1 contain similar language. Isaiah saw an oracle about Babylon, while Nahum saw one concerning Nineveh. The "formula" for both is the same. The Lord often works and presents His Word to us using familiar patterns. Another significant item about Nahum 1:1 is that it clearly states that Nahum was a real person. Nahum means "comforter." Some scholars have suggested that Nahum was not a historical person but merely a name used for the theme of the book—comfort. However, just as Isaiah was a historical person, so too was Nahum.

4. Israel's worship of the golden calf was a breach of the covenant the Lord God had made with her. The people of Israel deserved nothing but judgment and destruction. Yet in Exodus 34 the Lord reestablishes His covenant with His people. The Lord has mercy upon them. In Nahum, with the threat of the Assyrians upon the Lord's people, it must have seemed as if the Lord had abandoned them or was going to punish them through the hand of the Assyrians. By alluding to Exodus 34 and the reestablishment of the covenant with Israel, Nahum is reminding the people that the Lord has not abandoned them and will deliver them from their enemy.

5. The Lord is the divine warrior who will take vengeance upon the enemies of His people. He walks in the whirlwind and storm. He walks on the clouds as people walk on the dust of the ground. Mountains wither and quake before Him. He makes the sea dry, which is not only a reference to the Lord's power, but also to the way He

dried the Red Sea so His people could escape on dry ground (Exodus 14:21). The mountains melt, perhaps a reference to volcanoes. The enemies of the Lord will experience His almighty power as wrath and punishment.

6. The Bible provides many examples of people plotting against the Lord. For instance, in Genesis 11 the peoples conspired together to make a tower to reach into the heavens. The people plotted against the Lord. Certainly, the crucifixion of Jesus was a plot against the Lord. Many times, these plots are first directed against His people, His Church. To plot against a child of God is to plot against the Lord. To plot against His Church is to plot against the Lord. Individually, we also plot against the Lord when we consciously decide to sin.

7. One aspect of drunkenness is indulging in more. Just as drunkenness leads to more drunkenness, sin increases sin. Just as drunkenness alters the mind and distorts reality, so does sin. The sinner cannot think clearly about the things of God. Here in Nahum, Nineveh is "drunk" and the Lord will destroy her. Nineveh's powerful soldiers will be rendered powerless before the Lord, like a drunkard entangled in his or her drink.

8. The Lord's enemies are sin, death, and the devil, as well as those who side with them. Christ Jesus has defeated the power of sin by remaining sinless in temptation and the power of death by rising again. He cast Satan out of heaven so that he can no longer accuse us before the Father. The yoke and burden placed upon us by sin, death, and the devil have been shattered. We know that, in Christ Jesus, the victory is ours. Now we bear the yoke of Jesus, which is easy and light.

9. Isaiah also spoke of beautiful feet (Isaiah 52:7–8). In the context of Nahum, the messenger who brings news of Nineveh's destruction has beautiful feet because he is announcing that Jerusalem will have peace, for her enemy is destroyed. Jesus proclaimed that the kingdom of God was near. He healed the sick, raised the dead, and proclaimed the Good News of God. Jesus announced the time of the Lord's favor. Mary heard the Good News proclaimed by Jesus. She had her sins forgiven and worshiped Him by anointing His feet with perfume.

10. Today, Jesus appoints messengers to go and proclaim His Word and to deliver His forgiving gifts to His people. Those called to proclaim the Word of God publicly are pastors. The fields are ripe but the laborers are few. The Lord tells us to pray that more laborers be

sent out. The Church has a responsibility to continue to prepare and train men for the office of pastor. This is a God-given responsibility. Without pastors, without someone who is sent, people will not be able to hear the Good News of Jesus.

Lesson 2

The Lord's Judgment of Nineveh

Theme verse: *"For the* LORD *is restoring the majesty of Jacob as the majesty of Israel."*

Nahum 2:2

Objectives

By the power of the Holy Spirit working through God's Word, we will:

- see that the wicked belong to the Lord and that He uses them for His purpose.
- recognize that the Lord works through means.
- discover how the Lord uses history for the benefit of His Church.

11. Martin Luther in his sermons on John 15 explains well how the Lord uses evil for good:

"He who is able to learn, therefore, let him learn, in order that when afflicted and assailed everyone may conclude that the world, the devil, death, and all misfortune are only God's hoe and clipper; that all the revilement and disgrace the Christian experiences is God's way of fertilizing him. Then let him say: 'Praise God, who can use the devil and his malice to serve our good!' Otherwise—if his evil will had a free hand—he would soon kill us with his knife, and stifle and suffocate us with his stench. But now God takes him in hand and says: 'Devil, you are indeed a murderer and an evildoer; but I will use you for My purpose. You shall be My hoe; the world and your following shall be My manure for the fertilization of My vineyard.' We must surely acknowledge Him a great Master, who knows how to employ the devil's and all the world's wickedness for the vine's good and not for its harm and ruin, as these intend. This is what He says about it: 'Your intentions are evil indeed; you are very bitter and angry, and you plot to destroy My vine; but I will and must use you as My tools with which to cultivate and dress the vine. Therefore cut, chop, and hoe away, but not beyond the bounds that I set. For you shall go just so far that it will not ruin My vine but will help and improve it. You shall not fertilize it with manure until it is choked; you shall use only enough to make it sturdy and lush'" (AE 24:195).

12. The majesty of Jacob and Israel ultimately found restoration in the New Testament Church. The Church is the new Israel and the place where the Lord's salvation is found. Christians should not look to the modern nation of Israel or for the rebuilding of the temple in Jerusalem as the majesty of Israel, as some propose.

13. In popular culture, there are stories of thieves turning on thieves. There are accounts of prisoners exacting justice on worse criminals, such as prisoners severely beating or killing child molesters. While we should not rejoice in such things or encourage them, these are all examples of the Lord using evil to punish evil. The Lord uses a nation that perhaps goes to war for unjust reasons to punish another nation for the evil it has done.

14. Christians have hope even when all human help fails. The greatest example of this is death. Christians have hope through the resurrection of their Lord Jesus. Faith is hope in things unseen. While we may not understand why certain events happen in our lives, we have the Lord's promise that He will work them out for our good.

15. After Adam and Eve sinned in Genesis 3:7, they made clothing for themselves, because they were ashamed. Commenting on Genesis 3:7, Martin Luther wrote, "Therefore this is an excellent description of the corruption which has taken the place of original righteousness and glory. It was glory for man not to realize that he was naked. Moreover, what can be a greater depravity than that the nakedness which formerly was a glory is now turned into the greatest disgrace? No one blushes because of healthy and sound eyes. Distorted or weak eyes are regarded as less becoming and bring on shame. So in the state of innocence it was most honorable to go about naked. Now, after sin, when Adam and Eve see that they are naked, they are made ashamed, and they look for girdles with which to cover their disgrace. Yet how

much greater disgrace is there in this, that the will is impaired, the intellect depraved, and the reason entirely corrupt and altogether changed! Is this what they mean when they say that our natural endowments are perfect?" (AE 1:165).

We feel shame because, on some level, all people know they are sinful.

16. In 2 Kings 18:17–32, the Assyrians mocked the inhabitants of Jerusalem. In Nahum, the mockery of the Assyrians is turned against them. How the mighty have fallen!

17. Just as prey cannot escape from the lion on its own, we cannot escape from our adversaries on our own. The Lord compares our enemies (the devil, the world, and our sinful flesh) to a lion, because on our own, we cannot escape, resist temptation, or be delivered. We learn to rely on our Lord Jesus for rescue and salvation.

18. When the Lord is against you, none of your plans or ways will prosper. There is nothing more frightening, there is no greater judgment, than for the Lord to be against you. When the Lord is against you, all human efforts will fail.

19. The Lord has established government to thwart evil and to punish evildoers. Governments create police forces and armies to protect their citizens. Without the institution of government, anarchy and chaos would reign—something that is seen after the disruption of a government due to natural disasters and such. Even evil and corrupt governments manage to punish evildoers. However, the Lord judges corrupt governments after a time, bringing them to ruin. The Lord hides His justice behind or beneath government to punish the wicked and to restrain evil in the world. This is to say, the Lord works through means.

20. Just as the Lord uses means to punish evil, He uses means to dispense His mercy. The prime example of this is found in the preaching of His Word and the administration of the Sacraments. Through the spoken Word, Jesus comes to His people. Through the means of water and the Word, the Lord marks a person as His child. Through the means of bread and wine connected with His instituting Word, the Lord bestows His body and blood to eat and to drink for the forgiveness of sins.

The Lord uses Christians, in particular, as His instruments to dispense His kindness, goodness, and mercy to each other and to those in the world. In Matthew 25, Jesus tells His people that when they do a work of mercy to their neighbor, they are doing it to Him. Christians are masks of Jesus; He hides behind the Christian. The Christian becomes the hand or mouth of Jesus showing His love and mercy to his or her neighbor.

Lesson 3

Woe over Nineveh

Theme verse: *"Woe to the bloody city."*

Nahum 3:1

Objectives

By the power of the Holy Spirit working through God's Word, we will:

- see how fierce the Lord's judgment is against His enemies.
- believe that Jesus has taken the Lord's judgment upon Himself on the cross.
- take comfort in how the Lord delivers His people.

21. Many passages in the Bible speak of being "remembered no more." See Psalms 83:4; 88:5; and Jeremiah 11:19; two key passages are Jeremiah 31:34 and Ezekiel 21:32. A person can be in one of two conditions before the Lord. Either the Lord will no longer remember the person, or the Lord will no longer remember his or her sin. If the Lord does not remember you, you are in hell. If the Lord no longer remembers your sin, you are forgiven. The forgetting of Assyria is total judgment.

22. The repetition of themes is to ensure that the hearer understands—whether for good or bad. The Lord retells His judgment against the wicked to work repentance, to taunt the wicked, and to comfort His people. In a similar manner, the Lord retells the salvation of His people in several different ways. The Lord does the same in His Church. In the Divine Service, you hear that you are forgiven in the Absolution. In the sermon, you hear what Christ has done for you and that your sins are forgiven. In Holy Baptism, water is poured on your head to forgive your sins. In Holy Communion, forgiveness is put in

your mouth. The Lord utilizes all your senses to deliver His forgiveness to you. An analogy to everyday life might be this: How many different ways do you speak or show love to your spouse?

23. Leviticus 17:11 states, "For the life of the flesh is in the blood." When the Lord demands judgment, He demands blood. This is why animals were sacrificed in the Old Testament. This is why Christ suffered on the cross. He shed His blood for our sin. His blood was offered in place of ours. The Assyrians are judged and their blood is demanded. Also, the Assyrians wickedly shed innocent blood; now in judgment, their blood is demanded.

24. Public sin encourages more sin. It must be addressed more quickly. Evil done in the open causes the people to cry out to the Lord for deliverance. The Lord restrains evil and hears the cries of His people.

25. Prostitution is the selling of one's body for money, goods, or services. When a person sins, he or she is selling, so to speak, his or her body, mind, and spirit for an instant of gratification, wealth, or some such thing. Every time a person sins, he or she breaks the First Commandment to have no other gods. The Lord frequently compares sinning against Him to prostitution, particularly if it is the sin of idolatry. Every single sin makes something or someone into a god for us. Prostitution is also tainted and vile—it provokes a strong reaction in many people. The Lord wants to impress upon us how seriously He takes sin.

26. The Lord's anger is righteous and just. Once the human race fell into sin, nothing was deserved but judgment and punishment. The Lord owes us nothing. His judgment is fierce because He is righteous and He destroys sin. Seeing mass destruction and suffering should cause us to cry out for the Lord's mercy—no matter who suffers it. We know that we deserve that . . . and worse. What makes the judgment of God upon sinners particularly sad is that Jesus has taken the Lord's judgment upon Himself. Those who fall into judgment through unbelief essentially are telling Jesus, "Let me answer for my own sin."

27. In the writings of the prophets, the Lord's judgment often is called "the cup of wrath." Here the Lord makes people drunk on His wrath and continues to pour His wrath upon them until His cup is empty. The city of Nineveh will stagger like a drunkard under the Lord's wrath. In the garden, Jesus asked His Father to "remove this cup from Me" (Mark 14:36; Luke 22:42). The cup that Jesus was about

to receive was the cup of wrath, the Lord's judgment upon the entire world.

28. In Genesis, the Lord gave the blessing, "Be fruitful and multiply" (Genesis 1:28; 9:1). The Lord blesses His people with children. In societies that were under the Lord's judgment, the birth rate and population declined. In some cases, it was due to child sacrifice. In any case, part of being wiped out, removed from memory, is the elimination of a population. There are parallels for this today. The birthrate of most Western nations is declining. The popular message today is that we must control the world's population. This, in fact, turns what the Lord has called good—being fruitful and multiplying—into evil. If we as a people or society continue to despise the gifts of the Lord, He may well take them away from Western civilization and us.

29. Here, almost any example a person mentions will work. Are you afraid of the economy, sickness, war, and such? Do you fear for the Church? Any number of things can make us afraid and cause us to lose courage.

30. We need not be afraid, for our Lord has promised to work things for our good. The Lord delivered His people in the past and He continues to do so. In Nahum, the Assyrians were threatening to destroy the Lord's people, yet the tables were turned and Israel's enemy was destroyed. Ultimately, the Book of Nahum addresses how the Lord delivers His people from whatever can hurt or harm them.

Lesson 4

Is the Lord Just?

Theme verse: *"Look among the nations, and see; wonder and be astounded. For I am doing a work in your days that you would not believe if told."*

Habakkuk 1:5

Objectives

By the power of the Holy Spirit working through God's Word, we will:

- see that the Lord hears the cries of His people and answers their prayers.
- recognize that the Lord cares about the affairs of the earth and thwarts evil and injustice.
- learn that trials and temptations teach us to live a life of faith trusting in the promises of Christ.

31. Read Psalms 13:1 and 89:46. The psalmists and prophets customarily speak this way, asking the Lord how long it will be before He delivers His people as He has promised to do. People ask this question according to their station and vocation in life. A parent who is praying for a child to repent or come to faith may cry out, "How long, O Lord?" A pastor may cry out, "How long before Your Word works among Your people?" Luther describes Habakkuk's complaint in this way, "Here he begins to rebuke the people for their transgression and sin because of which the wrath of God and the burden had to come upon them. He introduces this with a passionate outcry and a supplication to God. It sounds as though he were angry with God because of His long-suffering with the sins of the people, which permitted them to transgress so smugly. It is as though he were saying:

'I am preaching much, but all to no avail. My words are despised, and no one mends his ways. On the contrary, people are getting worse all the time. Therefore I have no other recourse than to pour out my complaint to You" (AE 19:158). Whenever a person is long-suffering for the truth, it is appropriate to cry out to the Lord and ask, "How long?"

32. Many examples from the current day could be used. Any number of social issues could be raised. Use this question to encourage discussion.

33. The long answer to this question is the entire salvation history. The Lord giving the promise to Adam and Eve in the garden that He would crush the serpent's head, the call of Abraham, the flight of Israel out of Egypt, the crossing of the Red Sea, and so on. The ultimate culmination is the virgin birth of Jesus Christ and His suffering, death, and resurrection. Human reason would never have foreseen this to be how the Lord would save and rescue us from sin, death, and the power of the devil. Indeed, His ways are beyond us.

34. Luther writes, "The first sin, haughtiness over against other people, grieves the human heart; but the second sin, blasphemies against God, grieves the prophet and all saints far more" (AE 19:175).

35. The Holy Lord makes a holy people for Himself. Read 1 Peter 2:9, "You are a chosen race, a royal priesthood." To be holy is to be set apart. The Lord sets His people apart in the waters of Holy Baptism.

36. Luther has a great explanation: "These words of Habakkuk present the thoughts that occur to a struggling faith. It believes that God is just, but when He tarries so long and looks on the evil committed, faith is tempted to think that He is not just, but that He delights in these rogues. That is what we, too, are prone to think now that God permits our Gospel to be persecuted and reviled so miserably. . . . For it hurts exceedingly when the unrighteous prosper so long, earning their great good fortune, as it were, with their wrongs, and the righteous earn so much misfortune with their piety" (AE 19:180). Yet the Lord will punish the wicked and bless His people.

37. The ancient practice of giving up things for Lent was an exercise in self-control. The act of giving up something did not make a person more holy or earn favor with God, but it helped discipline the body and put to death our sinful nature that craves and lusts after all sorts of things. The Christian must be diligent to exercise self-control and to starve rather than feed his sinful nature.

38. Consider Habakkuk for a moment. He was preaching judgment against Israel, yet he also knew and believed that the Messiah would come according to the Lord's promise. Faith believes when there is no evidence to support it. The Lord loves to be captured in His promises. He loves for His people to pray, "O Lord, You have promised in Your Holy Word but I don't see evidence of this. Be faithful to Your Word."

39. St. Paul applies this passage from Habakkuk by equating the Jews who rejected Christ to the scoffers. The work the Lord did, which was not believed by the scoffers, was to raise up a descendent of David who did not see corruption (Jesus' body did not rot in the tomb). Those who believe in Christ receive the forgiveness of sins and freedom from the Law of Moses.

40. Christ faced every trial and temptation that is common to man. He suffered as a true man but was faithful and trusted completely in His Father for deliverance. 1 Corinthians 10:13 promises that the Lord will not allow us to be tempted beyond our ability to endure.

Lesson 5

The Lord's Justice Is Certain

Theme verse: *"The righteous shall live by his faith."*

Habakkuk 2:4b

Objectives

By the power of the Holy Spirit working through God's Word, we will:

- recognize that our righteousness comes by faith.
- see that the Lord uses external means to strengthen our faith.
- understand that the Lord's people have always been justified by faith.

41. The word *tablet* evokes the Law and the covenant the Lord God made with His people after He released them from Egypt and they camped near Mount Sinai. Just as the Lord made a covenant with His people when Moses brought the two tablets down from the mountain, so too is the Lord making or reestablishing His covenant by having Habakkuk's vision recorded on tablets. Luther notices a similarity between the use of tablets and the external elements in the Sacraments of Baptism and Holy Communion. He writes, "To strengthen faith, God usually adds an external feature or sign to the Word, which is similar to attaching a seal to a letter. Thus Jeremiah had to carry a wooden chain about his neck. . . . Also in the New Testament Baptism and the Sacrament were instituted as visible signs in addition to the Gospel. That is what Habakkuk, too, is doing here by divine command" (AE 19:192).

42. This threefold message—promise, exhortation, and threat—is basically the proper distinction between Law and Gospel. The threat of punishment drives us to seek forgiveness. The Lord promises us that

He will forgive our sins for Christ's sake. The exhortation teaches us about the Lord's Word, tells us what He has done for us, instructs us by telling us how the Lord has sustained the faith of His people in the past, and teaches us how to please Him. As Luther said, if the promise, exhortation, and threat (the preaching of the entire counsel of God) does not engender and strengthen faith, nothing will.

43. Righteousness is something that the Lord does. He is righteous and works righteousness in His people. His people receive righteousness by faith, that is, by receiving the gifts of the Lord. There is a way of speaking about faith that equates faith with Jesus. If you have faith, you receive righteousness. If you have Jesus, you have righteousness. This keeps both faith and righteousness as gifts and not as works of our own.

44. From the very beginning of salvation history, the Lord has taken the weak and lowly and glorified them to show that it is He at work and not man. Abraham was chosen by the Lord and made into a great nation. The lowly nation of Israel was chosen by the Lord to be His people and to shame Egypt. David killed Goliath. Ultimately, Christ Jesus demonstrates this. See Philippians 2:8: "He humbled Himself by becoming obedient to the point of death, even death on a cross."

45. When man fell into sin, all of creation was subjected to futility, as Romans 8 says. In Genesis, the Lord gave man dominion over creation. When man fell into sin, that dominion of man whereby creation served man willingly was lost. From that moment on, man grew crops by the sweat of his brow. He forced the earth and creation into submission through various means. Yet when the judgment of God comes, man's dominion is lost. In this case, the judgment against Babylon is so great that even the stones and wooden beams used to build her buildings cry out for the Lord to bring justice.

46. The world remembers Alexander the Great thousands of years after he conquered the world. It remembers the great Roman Empire. Even more will the deeds of the Lord be remembered. In fact, what the Lord accomplished by delivering His people in Christ Jesus is better known than any other event in history. Habakkuk has not only the destruction of the Babylonian Empire in mind but also the coming of Christ and His reign in glory. The destruction of the Babylonian Empire also demonstrates that the Lord is the Lord of history and in control of world events—even if the world does not acknowledge this.

47. The king of Babylon could not imagine being defeated. He had defeated all the powerful kingdoms in the world. He was confident in his ability to rule and in the power and skill of his armies. Yet his kingdom would also fall. As the saying goes, "Pride goes before a fall." In fact, the root of sin is often pride. Satan took pride in himself and attempted to storm heaven and usurp God's throne. It is no surprise that the people Satan tempts follow a similar path.

48. In the Scriptures, when people enter into the presence of God, they are usually silent—silent due to fear. Remember that Adam and Eve hid from the presence of God. Even the apostle John, when he encountered the presence of the glorified Jesus in the Book of Revelation, fell on his face. The hymn "Let All Mortal Flesh Keep Silence" reminds us that as we go to Holy Communion, we are entering the presence of the crucified, risen, and glorified God, who gives us His true body and blood to eat and to drink for the forgiveness of sins. It is truly awesome. So the recognition of His presence and that we poor miserable sinners do not deserve a gracious Lord is good; yet He invites us to come to Him. He hides His glory, power, and might behind the bread and wine. Our Lord dwells among His people.

49. Faith receives the righteousness of God. Because of faith we are credited or accounted righteous. This is nothing other than forensic justification. The Lord declares us righteous and faith clings to that Word. The Lord not only declares us righteous but actually makes us righteous. In faith, we receive the active and passive righteousness of Jesus. We do not earn His favor, but have received it because of the Gospel of Jesus Christ.

50. Some have this notion that the Old Testament presented a works-righteous religion full of commandments and sacrifices, whereas the New Testament offers a religion of grace. The reality is that the Lord has always saved His people by grace through faith. Habakkuk proclaims that the righteous live by faith. Abraham was accounted righteous by faith. The way of salvation in the Old Testament is no different than that of the New Testament: faith in the promise of God. The only difference is the perspective of time: before or after the cross. Before the cross, faith looks forward towards it. After the cross, faith looks back at what Jesus did and accomplished. Faith receives the gifts of Christ.

Lesson 6

Habakkuk's Prayer

Theme verse: *"Yet I will rejoice in the LORD; I will take joy in the God of my salvation."*

Habakkuk 3:18

Objectives

By the power of the Holy Spirit working through God's Word, we will:

- take joy in the God of our salvation in the midst of hardship and suffering.
- pray the Psalms as if they were our prayers.
- believe that the greater our hardships are, the greater the Lord's deliverance will be for us.

51. In Habakkuk's prayer in chapter 3, he borrows liberally from the Psalms. Because of this, some liberal critical scholars have suggested that Habakkuk did not write this prayer at all, suggesting instead that it was pieced together from the Psalms. Indeed, Habakkuk's prayer resembles the pattern found in the Psalms because he prays them as if they were his own prayer. Under the inspiration of the Holy Spirit, Habakkuk indeed used phrases from the Psalms as he wrote his prayer about the salvation of God. Yet this chapter is more than a piecemeal composition of various psalms. It is Habakkuk's psalm of joy at the Lord's deliverance of His people. Habakkuk's psalm was used in the worship of the Jewish people, just as the Psalms were. In the Psalms and in Habakkuk 3, the Lord is reminded how He saved His people in times past. The psalmists and Habakkuk recall the mighty deeds of the Lord. We too can pray the Psalms as if they were our prayers. We pray, reminding the Lord how He saved His people in

the flood, how He delivered His people out of Egypt, and how He saved His people from their sins in Jesus. "Lord, just as You saved Your people in the past, save me now" (Hosanna). This is a prayer of faith.

52. Many people think that the *kyrie eleison* ("Lord, have mercy") is only a confession of sins or a request for forgiveness. While "Lord, have mercy" indeed may be a plea for forgiveness, it is much more. In the Divine Service, typically, the Confession of sins and the Absolution precede the *kyrie eleison*. Because of this, some people have asked, "Why are we asking for forgiveness twice in a row?" But this is not what is happening. In the flow of the service, because the Lord's people have been forgiven, they cry to the Lord for mercy, that is, to save them now from whatever is hurting or harming them. This use of the prayer "Lord, have mercy" is biblical. Throughout the Bible, people cry, "Lord, have mercy," not primarily for the forgiveness of sins but for deliverance from whatever is troubling them at that moment. When you pray the *kyrie eleison*, you are praying to be relieved from whatever is troubling you. And when something is too terrible for words, pray, "Lord, have mercy."

53. Teman and Mount Paran were places along Israel's journey through the wilderness into the Promised Land. This is the salvation history of the Lord's people. Habakkuk is retelling the story of their deliverance. Salvation for the Lord's people occurred at both of these places. Just as the Lord provided salvation at Teman and Mount Paran, He provides salvation and deliverance for His people today. Note that the earth is full of His praise; this is a twofold praise, first from the Lord's people who were being delivered, then from all of creation, for the deliverance of the Lord's people will bring about the deliverance of all creation (Romans 8:19).

54. The glory of the Lord described here is not the splendor of creation, the majesty of the mountains, and such; it is that of His almighty power to save His people. Oftentimes, people think of the Lord God as being distant from them, "up there" in the heavens. These verses from Habakkuk show us that the Lord is not "up there" in some distant place, but with His people, helping them and delivering them. These verses show us that the Lord is near to His people. The glory of the Lord displayed here is the salvation of His people.

55. The Lord's glory can be displayed in one of two ways: it can be manifest in His power and might, or it can be hidden in the means

the Lord uses to save His people. When the Lord displays His glory to the enemies of the Lord's people, they are destroyed—they see destruction and death. At the same time, the Lord's people see their deliverance and salvation. Often in Scripture, the Lord's favor toward you is the destruction of your enemies, particularly the enemies that are sin, death, and Satan.

56. Natural disasters are the result of Adam's fall into sin. Because of sin, the natural processes of this world and of the cosmos do not operate perfectly. Yet there are other aspects of natural disasters. Creation itself, being subjected to futility (Romans 8:20–21), groans for the coming of the Lord. Creation itself does not want to be burdened by sin and reacts against the misuse of the Lord's good creation. Natural disasters reflect the Lord's general judgment over sin. Yet as Matthew 24 and Romans 8 indicate, these natural disasters, earthquakes and such, are signs that we live in the last days. For the Christian, the end of the world is not a frightening matter; rather, it is our deliverance from sin and death. On the Last Day, our Lord Jesus will come to raise those who have died, to restore creation to its sinless splendor, and to dwell among His people forever. This is the salvation of the Lord's people.

57. The Lord is the subject of the verbs. The credit for the battle and victory belongs to the Lord, not Israel. The arrows fired against the enemy were the Lord's arrows. The Lord marched through the earth. The Lord crushed the head of the wicked. When it comes to salvation, the action and work is entirely the Lord's, not ours.

58. The greater the threat or the greater the trial, suffering, or distress, the greater the Lord's salvation will be. So the larger the challenge, the greater the deliverance will be. Throughout the Old Testament, the people of Israel encountered enemies that they of themselves could not defeat, yet they were victorious—not because of their own reason or strength, but because the Lord fought for them. So when a Christian is confronted with an impossible situation, he should take comfort in the certainty of faith that the Lord will provide a way of escape. The Lord will provide deliverance and salvation. The Christian already knows the final outcome; we will be raised on the Last Day and spend eternity with the Lord in the new heaven and new earth. In the course of our lives, we will face challenges, trials, temptations, and suffering that may strike us with temporary setbacks,

ultimately even our physical death. However, we know the final outcome and we know that the Lord will never leave or forsake us.

59. In the midst of challenges and trials, the psalmist and Habakkuk take joy in the salvation the Lord will provide. Knowing for certain that the Lord will deliver you provides not only comfort but also joy. The Virgin Mary, upon hearing that the promised Messiah was to be born, took joy in the salvation of her Lord.

60. Quite simply, Jesus had joy of the cross because He was saving us. Jesus received joy in the midst of suffering separation from His Father, because He knew that His people would be saved by His death and resurrection. Imagine that—Jesus took joy in thinking of your salvation while He suffered on the cross. He also took joy in obeying the will of His Father. What an amazing Lord we have.

Lesson 7

The Lord Judges Judah

Theme verse: *"The great day of the LORD is near, near and hastening fast."*

Zephaniah 1:14a

Objectives

By the power of the Holy Spirit working through God's Word, we will:

- see how preaching builds on the message the Church has always proclaimed, on the foundation of the prophets and the apostles.
- learn that reformation, renewal, and revitalization of the Church always begins with repentance and forgiveness.
- believe that the great day of the Lord is near and hastening so that the Lord can bring us His salvation.

61. Zephaniah followed in a long line of prophets that began with Moses, fulfilling Deuteronomy 18:15–17. Zephaniah indicates that his great-great-grandfather is Hezekiah, one of the good kings of Judah, who initiated reforms in the Church. Josiah would have been a relative of Zephaniah. Before the fall, man had communion with the Lord. After the fall, His holy presence not only terrified but threatened to destroy sinful man. Through the prophets, the Lord mediated His Word, both the Law and the Gospel, through a human voice and with human words. Yet the prophets did not speak their own words but the Word of the Lord. The ultimate fulfillment of Deuteronomy 18 is found in Christ Jesus.

62. Pastors today continue in the line of the prophets, prophesying, that is, preaching, the Word of God to the Lord's people.

Like the prophets, pastors are to proclaim not their own words but the Word of God. As with the prophets, the Lord uses pastors to mediate His Word to His people with human voice and words.

63. In Genesis 6, the wickedness of man was so great and so permeated creation that the Lord repented (grieved) that He had ever made man. Imagine that: man's wickedness and the intent of his evil heart caused the Lord to wish that He had never made man. So the Lord decided to destroy man and all the living creatures on the land, except the eight souls (Noah and his family) and the animals on the ark. Even with the "day of the LORD" (the flood) near and hastening quickly, the Lord's patience gave the world 120 years to heed Noah's preaching. In Zephaniah 1:2, the Lord through the prophet declares His judgment, "I will utterly sweep away everything." The announcement of severe and total judgment is intended to shock the people into recognizing the seriousness of their sin and to prompt repentance. As the Lord did in the time of the flood, Zephaniah threatens total destruction not only of man but also of every living thing on the earth. Lest anyone think the Lord is reneging on His promise not to destroy the earth in Genesis 9:15, note that there the Lord promised to never again destroy the earth with a flood. Other means of destroying the earth are still available to Him. The initial application of this prophecy was the Babylonian captivity. It also has an eschatological application—judgment on the Last Day.

64. This is a sort of chiasm: Destroy Man—Destroy Creatures on Earth—Destroy Man. Not only will man be wiped out, but all that is necessary to support him in his body also will be wiped out. When Adam and Eve sinned, God cursed creation (Romans 8:19–20). In Genesis 9, the Lord instilled the fear of man into animals. The Lord did this to protect creation from sinful man. The perfection of creation was lost when man sinned. Although Christ died on the cross to redeem mankind from sin and death, when He returns in glory He will also restore creation—remaking the heavens and the earth—purified from sin.

65. Quite simply, it was idolatry. In verse 4, Baal worship is mentioned. Although King Josiah did not tolerate Baal worship and cut down the high places, there was still a "remnant" of Baal worshipers. The Lord threatened to remove the Baal worshipers from the land. The Babylonian captivity effectively removed Baal worship from Judah and Israel for good. In reference to the idolaters, Psalm 9:5 says, "You

have blotted out their name forever and ever." Zephaniah 1:5 speaks of those who bow down to the host of the heavens and Milcom, the god of the Ammonites (1 Kings 11:5, 33). *Milcom* contains the Hebrew root for the word *king*. In either case, putting one's trust in Milcom, the god of the Ammonites, or the king is forbidden. Keep in mind that Zephaniah's prophecy is based on the lost book (Deuteronomy) that had been found. Deuteronomy 17:3 forbids the worship of the sun, moon, or any of the host of heaven. The Lord is threatening judgment because of the idolatry in Judah.

66. The Day of the Lord is full of wrath for the enemies of the Lord and His Church. On the other hand, the Day of the Lord is full of mercy for the people of God. On the Day of the Lord, the Lord comes to bring salvation to His people. 1 Thessalonians 5:2 says that the Day of the Lord will come like a "thief in the night." Verse 8 of the same book and chapter says to have a "breastplate of faith and love" and "for a helmet the hope of salvation." Most frequently, Scripture says to remain "awake" and to not become complacent with the world. The Christian prepares for the "day of the LORD" by remaining in the faith and trusting in the promises of Jesus. This involves confessing one's sins and receiving His forgiveness bestowed through His forgiving gifts.

67. All Christian preaching is summarized by Mark 1:15, "Repent and believe in the Gospel." This is the preaching of the Law and the Gospel. Ever since humans fell into sin, preaching has taught "repent and believe in the Gospel," that is, believe in the promise and deliverance of God. The Law of God does not change. The Gospel or promise of God does not change. Zephaniah did not invent a new message. He preached what the Book of Deuteronomy taught. Many people today want an updated message rather than "repent and believe in the Gospel." The temptation always is to add to or subtract from the Word of God.

68. To those who are unprepared and unexpectant, the day of the Lord always will be soon and near. In his 1525 commentary on Zephaniah, Martin Luther writes, "He is always opposed to the proud who contradict him, against the smug people who hold him in contempt, who kept on accusing the prophet of lying. . . . Therefore, the prophet keeps on pressing home the coming calamity in great detail and with great vehemence. You see, as we have said before, they felt smug, they had no fear for themselves, they were confirmed in their

false idea. But so it happens with the wicked. When they reach full flower and have complete control, when nothing seems less possible than their destruction, then sudden destruction comes to them. As the prophet says in the psalm, they will not live out half their days (Ps. 55:23). And Christ also says in His Gospel parable of the unjust servant (Luke 12:46) that the master will come when the servant is not thinking it. You see, because they remain stubborn, the threats of the Lord move them not at all. Therefore destruction comes to them suddenly and unexpectedly" (AE 18:333).

On the other hand, those who are waiting eagerly for the coming of the Lord may wonder what is taking Him so long. This especially is true of those who are suffering. In Revelation 6:10, the martyrs cry out, "How long before You will judge and avenge our blood on those who dwell on the earth?" To those who wait in expectation, the coming of the Lord seems like a long time. While no one knows the day or hour of Christ's return (Matthew 24:36), Jesus gave His disciples signs that would indicate that the time was near (false Christs, wars, rumors of wars, earthquakes, darkening of the sky, etc.). Revelation 22:20 concludes, "Surely I am coming soon." The saints reply, "Come, Lord Jesus!"

69. For those being judged, the coming of the kingdom of God is Law (judgment and punishment). For those being saved, the coming of the kingdom of God is Gospel (deliverance and salvation). On the Last Day when Christ returns in His glory, those who believe in Him will be raised to life and be with Him forever (Gospel). Those who did not believe will be raised to everlasting punishment (Law).

70. Ever since the fall, all mankind is corrupt, sinful, and in a state of rebellion against God. Out of the lost and condemned human race, the Lord calls and gathers His Church. His Church is a minority in the world; it lives under the cross and suffers from various afflictions both internal and external. Because of the corruption of mankind, errors enter the Church. At various times within the life of the Church, the Lord raises up prophets, teachers, and pastors to bring about a reformation of the Church. Each reformation, renewal, and revitalization of the Church begins with repentance. "Repent and believe in the Gospel." Even when error enters into the Church, the error is never total. The gates of hell will not prevail against the Church. The Church will remain until Christ returns. Philip Melanchthon, author of the Augsburg Confession, the Apology to the

Augsburg Confession, and the Power and Primacy of the Pope in the Book of Concord, summarized this as the four laws of Church history.

Melanchthon's Four Laws of Church History	
1	General corruption and apostasy of mankind
2	The Church is a minority or remnant in the world
3	Reformation—Church history is a series of reformations
4	Of eschatology or of relativity—error and corruption never total in the Church

Reformation, renewal, and revitalization of the Church always goes back to "repent and believe in the Gospel." Zephaniah went back to Deuteronomy. Martin Luther began the Reformation by calling for repentance. The same is true today. The only way to revitalize the Church is to go back to repenting and receiving the forgiveness of the Gospel.

Lesson 8

The Lord Judges the Nations

Theme verse: *"Seek the LORD, all you humble of the land, who do His just commands; seek righteousness; seek humility; perhaps you may be hidden on the day of the anger of the LORD."*

Zephaniah 2:3

Objectives

By the power of the Holy Spirit working through God's Word, we will:

- seek the Lord while He may be found in His Word and Sacraments.
- see that judgment began with Jesus on the cross, where Jesus consumed the wrath of God.
- learn to entrust our souls into the hands of our faithful Creator in times of suffering and trial.

71. When a nation or culture calls what is good and right, bad and evil, while exalting what the Lord calls wicked as good, that nation or culture is truly shameless. Sin and wickedness have so thoroughly corrupted that the culture collectively or a person individually does not even know that they should feel shame for their actions (Romans 1:28). Many examples could be given from the media, television, movies, and such.

72. The nations and peoples that the Lord is judging and destroying are arrogant and proud. In some cases, these peoples or nations believe that the Lord should have made them His chosen people. In so doing, these peoples have made other gods (imagined and fantasy gods who did make them their people). On the other hand, the humble recognize that they are nothing but beggars before the

Lord. The humble know that they deserve nothing but wrath and judgment from the Lord, but humbly seek His mercy where He has located it for them to find. The Lord can be sought in His mercy and in His forgiving gifts, that is, in the preaching of His Word, in Holy Absolution, Holy Baptism, and Holy Communion. We seek the Lord in Jesus, crucified and risen for us. This is to seek the Lord in His righteousness, the righteousness of Jesus.

73. The Lord did restore Judah from captivity in Babylon. This is the immediate fulfillment. This section also points forward to the kingdom of Christ. When Christ Jesus was born, the Lord was "mindful of them." Luther writes, "Then the Lord will redeem them. Their captivity will not last forever. Thus the prophets everywhere very diligently exercise care that they do not cast out the people of Judah completely, as if they were never to be restored. You see, no matter how hard they press the captivity and whatever is still to come upon the people, yet the prophets still have their eyes fixed on the kingdom of Christ which is to come. They knew that kingdom would come from that people. . . . Therefore it was necessary that, if not all, then a few, be saved. So then, by the counsel of God, many were led back out of Babylon into their land" (AE 18:342).

74. While the Lord brought judgment to the nations, He also brought salvation in Christ Jesus. Revelation 7:9 says "a great multitude that no one could number, from every nation, from all tribes and peoples and languages, standing before the throne and before the Lamb." Christ Jesus came to redeem all people. Luther writes, "You see, this was, as it were, a sort of prelude for the coming kingdom of Christ, which was going to spread not merely among the Jews but into the whole world, throughout all nations. Afterwards the apostles established and spread that kingdom, so that it then began to shine almost everywhere, even among the heathen. Therefore Christ brought it about that people everywhere worshiped the Lord, not just in Jerusalem but among all nations. That is what the prophet is saying here about the worship of God being spread even among the heathen: 'All the islands of the nations' will bow down to Him. That is, they will offer their gifts in the temple at Jerusalem. Even the heathen will bear witness that this is the worship of the true God" (AE 18:344).

75. Proverbs 16:18 says, "Pride goes before destruction." Not only does this occur in people's day-to-day lives, but also in our life before the Lord. Satan fell from the Lord's grace over pride. It long has

been suggested that Satan felt human beings were inferior creatures to the angels and that he resented serving these “lesser” beings. His pride caused him to rebel against the Lord and be cast from grace. Likewise, Adam’s and Eve’s pride caused them to think more highly of their own opinions than the Lord’s sure and certain Word. So it has gone through the history of mankind up to the present day. Pride causes us to question the Lord and His Word and to rebel.

76. “The prophet Zephaniah says exactly the same thing here. You see, he is subjecting all nations to the wrath of God and to the captivity, lest they think that only the people of God have merited captivity. Yet the Lord does begin first of all with His own people, as Peter says in 1 Peter 4:17: ‘For the time has come for judgment to begin with the household of God; and if it begins with us, what will be the end of those who do not believe the Gospel of God?’ You see, after He has sent out His Word, He first crucifies His own martyrs and preachers of the Word. He makes His own people suffer many trials. Then, after He has afflicted the righteous for some time, the terrible wrath and punishment of God soon comes against the enemies of the Word and of the people of God. This is what we, too, are experiencing today” (AE 18:344–345).

77. The loss of dominion over creation was part of the curse the Lord placed upon Adam and Eve after the fall. Yet in the curse, the loss of dominion was not total. Human beings still have the ability to shape creation, move mountains, herd animals, and so on. Yet there are times when dominion is lost or greatly diminished. In times of “natural” disaster—earthquakes, tsunamis, hurricanes, tornados, and such—we see that dominion has been lost.

78. Indeed, the saints of the Lord and the martyrs cry to the Lord, asking how long they must wait before judgment will come upon their persecutors. The Church prays for all to repent and be saved, but if hearts are hardened and repentance will not come, then the Church prays for deliverance. The deliverance can either come through the repentance of the Church’s enemy or through his or her judgment and destruction. The Church and the people of God indeed can and should rejoice in their deliverance, even if that deliverance comes as evil is destroyed.

79. The Father executed His wrath for the sins of the world on His Son, Jesus Christ. The Father began in His own house with His Son. In Hebrews 12:3, Jesus endured hostility against Himself. Jesus

was disciplined for our sins. We as the disciples of Jesus should not be surprised that we have suffering in our lives, since our master Jesus also did (not on His own account but on our account).

80. “That is, those whom God afflicts with suffering which they themselves have not sought and chosen should entrust their souls to Him. They do well, continue in good works, do not withdraw because of the suffering, and entrust themselves to their Creator, who is faithful. This is a great comfort for us. God created your soul without any trouble and assistance on your part. He did so before you came into being. Accordingly, He is surely able to preserve it. Therefore entrust it to Him, but in such a way that it is done with good works” (AE 30:130–131).

Lesson 9

The Day of the Lord Is Restoration

Theme verse: *"The LORD has taken away the judgments against you; He has cleared away your enemies. The King of Israel, the LORD, is in your midst; you shall never again fear evil."*

Zephaniah 3:15

Objectives

By the power of the Holy Spirit working through God's Word, we will:

- rejoice and delight in the promises of Jesus.
- pray that the Lord would deliver us from all evil.
- delight in how the Lord uses the weak and the lowly things of this world—how He has chosen you and me.

81. The city is guilty of rebelling against the Word of God. When the Word of God is despised, the Lord takes it away. Since the Lord is present in His Word, to have it removed is to have the presence of God depart from us. Rebelling against the Word of God effectively tells the Lord that we no longer wish to be His people. We no longer want Him to be our God. Read Deuteronomy 9:7, 24. The people of Israel had a history of being rebellious, as do we according to our sinful nature. The condemnations against the rebellious city apply to all who rebel.

82. The Lord's people were to be holy, that is, set apart from the other peoples of the lands. This is why the Lord forbade them from intermarrying. This is why the Lord gave strict sexual morals—to set His people apart and keep them holy. A holy people live holy lives. So, Israel's enemy, the Ammonites, arise from incest between a father and

a daughter. Back before the flood in Genesis 6:2–4, the sons of God married the sons of men, because they found the women attractive. This has nothing to do with angels marrying humans or with extraterrestrial aliens marrying humans. This is a story of the Lord's people having mixed marriages with a people who did not belong to the Lord. This was a plague that infected Israel (and the Church) from the start. The Lord found His city defiled. The priests were unable to perform their priestly duties because they were unclean due to mixed marriages (Ezra and Nehemiah). The people in the city were defiled and had mixed true worship with false worship, true religion with pagan worship. His city was unclean; it was no longer holy.

83. Ultimately, the "LORD within her is righteous" refers to Christ. He is righteous and dwells with His people in His Church. Luther writes, "He is speaking about Christ Jesus, the Savior, who, unlike them, teaches true righteousness. You see, the greatest wickedness was again in control when Christ came. Therefore He set Himself against their wickedness, etc." (AE 18:352).

84. The passage from Deuteronomy shows that the Lord delighting or rejoicing can be a Law or Gospel situation. The Lord in His righteous wrath and anger told Israel that He would delight in bringing ruin and destruction upon them. What horrible judgment! In the more frequent and comforting way, the Lord takes delight in His people—that is, He has plans to prosper them. He delights in fulfilling and being faithful to His promises.

85. The Lord makes His people "renowned and praised" by making them holy, by setting them apart as His people. The nations look at what the Lord did, wondering and marveling. The Lord delights in forgiving you and in blessing you.

86. At first glance, this is the undoing of the tower of Babel. The Lord confused the languages of the people because the people conspired against Him. There was evil on their lips. Pentecost undid the tower of Babel; everyone who heard the apostles preach heard the Gospel in his own language. The pure speech is the Gospel. The Lord places the Gospel upon our lips, purifying them from evil. In fact, the Gospel purifies our entire life so that the entire life of the believer is holy. Luther writes, "The prophet selects all his words in such a way that we can have no doubt that we must take them all to mean the Gospel. Thus he here is describing the invocation of the name of the Lord and the single-hearted worship of God as 'pure speech.'

Therefore the meaning is: 'I will remove those who corrupt their own deeds, who adulterate the Word of God, who use impure speech. I will establish a holy people for Myself. I will give them pure speech. . . . They will teach the sound and blameless Word of faith" (AE 18:356).

87. These are the Gentiles who came into the Church. The Gospel bears such fruit that even the Gentiles become grafted into the Lord's family. Christians are scattered throughout the entire world. Christ is present where two or three gather in His name.

88. The humble and lowly people inherit the kingdom of God. In fact, Jesus said the kingdom is theirs. Yet in this world, the Lord's Church—the humble and the meek—is under the cross. The Church does not appear impressive by worldly standards. Luther writes, "In few but very beautiful words he is describing the church of Christ, that it is a poor, needy, and oppressed people who call on the Lord and hope in the Lord. This is the greatest righteousness; this is the highest worship of God" (AE 18:358). This greatest righteousness and highest worship is nothing other than to receive the forgiveness of sins, to approach Christ as a poor beggar and receive His gifts.

89. Ultimately, we do not fear evil, because Jesus has conquered evil. Luther writes, "It is one thing to endure evil and another to fear evil, just as it is one thing to die and another to see or taste death, as Christ says in John (John 8:51). Thus the Law is dead as far as we are concerned when it has lost its power and sting. Then it can no longer frighten us; it no longer has the right to condemn us. In the same way, although death may come upon a just man, yet it cannot terrify him, nor can it exercise its tyranny against or upon him. Therefore to him death is more correctly a sleep" (AE 18:360).

90. In the Luke passage, Jesus rejoices in the Holy Spirit that the truth about Him was hidden from the wise and understanding and revealed to little children. This is the theology of the cross. The weak and the lowly find favor and receive the wisdom of Jesus. The wise, understanding, and powerful consider the cross foolishness. In the Hebrews passage, the joy set before Jesus was enduring the cross for you. He took joy in saving you. What an amazing Savior we have!